HEARERS GUILD OF THE WATCHERS
SPEAKERS SENSERS
PROPHETS

ESSENTIAL HANDBOOKS
FOR CHRISTIANS

VOL.
III

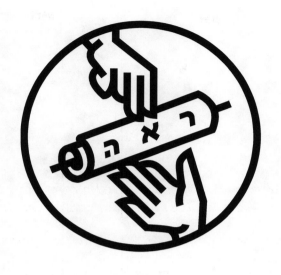

THE OFFICE

OF THE PROPHET

VOL.

III

ANDREW BILLINGS

WITH A FOREWORD BY: DON WOLABAUGH

CONTENTS

FOREWORD

Whether you are a young prophet trying to find your way, a prophet with a little training, or a seasoned prophet who has been flowing in your gift for some time, this book is a must-read!

The revelatory insight that Andrew Billings shares with us through years of experience and his own walk with God is outstanding. As a pastor of over 35 years I have been able to successfully navigate working with the strong prophetic voices in our house, and while reading this book I have been able to glean further very useful and helpful insights that had me saying "Wow that's amazing!"

Andrew Billings understanding of the collaborative work between the apostolic and the prophetic is amazing. Anyone on their prophetic journey can glean from the myriad of nuggets in this book allowing the reader to glean incredible truth.

Don Wolabaugh
Founder and Pastor of Harvest Chapel
Abbottstown PA

INTRODUCTION

Who is a prophet? And furthermore, what is it that makes a prophet? What are the characteristics of a prophet? Are you a prophet? Or is someone you know, work with, or are related to? What actually is a prophet, and what does that person do? How do we recognize them?

Welcome to volume three of the Guild of the Prophets. The previous two books in the series have introduced the prophetic as it applies to all of us as children of God. In this volume, we are going to introduce the specific role and calling of a prophet. We will explain the purpose and preparation of a prophet, while bringing understanding to why God created and designed the role of a prophet in the Old and New Testaments, as well as in the modern-day church.

The role of the prophet has easily become the most mis-understood and persecuted of all of the five apostolic roles in the church today. While there are many reasons for this misunderstanding, it is clear that mainly immature and reckless displays of the prophetic role have played a major part in the prophet's misrepresentation. However, as the body of Christ, we cannot afford to allow bad or poor operations of the prophetic office to lead us to discard something God has ordained for our benefit and His glory. We must address and rectify both the poor example of a prophet and the body of Christ's discardment of prophetic gifts. The prophet is, at every level of kingdom and secular community, essential to the well-being, guidance, focus, mission, and conscience of the bride of Christ.

Whether you feel that you are a prophet, called to be a prophet, or just interested in learning more about this role in the church, then this book is essential for you. For prophets, both young and seasoned, you will be taught (and reminded of) who you are, why you are the way you are, and introduced to deeper facets of your existing gifts while being awakened to other gifts you have not yet accessed. I pray this enlightens you to a higher standard of conduct and stewardship, so that as you grow and mature in your prophetic role, you are received and not discarded by the body of Christ.

For those who are reading volume three with a hunger to learn more of God's way in governing His church, you'll be given perspective into the prophet's role and function. This insight will begin to open up understanding as to why God has placed these jewels among us. You will be exposed to their greater function in the body of Christ, and to the necessity of prophets. This will cause a hunger to be birthed in you to assist the prophet in his or her growth so that the whole body can flourish into all that God is calling the local church to be.

Prophets are unique personalities. This volume will help us understand who we are and why we see and process things differently than others around us. It will help us more clearly understand our differences and highlight our many strengths. The truth is that your community needs you to be functioning in the capacity for which God designed you, and this book will take you deeper toward maturity and cause you to function in a way that will be a blessing to all around you. God has made you to be you—it is important to understand what part of you is God-designed and what part needs to be reshaped in order for God's design and plan to be best revealed in your life.

You are not called to look and function like a pastor or an evangelist. God has made you to function in your own way, according to the pattern and characteristics He has outlined in His Word. The world needs more true prophets today. Will this be you? As you read, open up your heart and allow God to raise you up and train you toward your high calling as a prophet of God, declaring all that He has placed in your heart.

The first volume served as an introduction to the extraordinary call of a prophet, but all the following volumes are going to take us much deeper. This is just the beginning for all God has for you.

CHAPTER 1

GOD'S HEART FOR THE PROPHETS: INTIMACY WITH GOD

Before we can properly understand the role of a prophet, we must first understand God's heart and perspective for the office of the prophet and the reason why He created the role of a prophet for the world, the church, and individuals.

Can you imagine, just for a moment, God dreaming over the church before it was actually birthed? Jesus would commission His team and have them wait in Jerusalem for the outpouring of the Holy Spirit, empowering them to be His witnesses throughout the earth. God, the supreme master architect of His church, looked at the bride of Christ through time and planned the perfect team to lead and equip, train and encourage—and even correct—so the church would have the ultimate strategy to be perfectly positioned to flourish and grow. We have been entrusted with the task of holding to God's intended design and spiritual DNA.

One of the many attributes I love and admire about God is His intricate attention to detail within details. Imagine the process that God went through as He designed the apostolic leadership of the New Testament church—the fivefold gifts to lead and serve the church. He saw pastors, teachers, evangelists, apostles, and prophets. He created roles that would be an answer to the need of the church for its guidance, nutrients, direction, instruction, vision, and nurturing. God understands the heart and need of the church, broken down to the intimate needs of each individual person within it, far more than we can even understand our own makeup.

Everything that God does has a purpose. He has multiple intentions for everything He creates, plans, and institutes. As humans, we often see a single purpose for an event in our lives, but God's ways and wisdom are far superior to anything we could ever grasp as humankind. At best, humanity's wisdom is haphazard compared to God's great design and wisdom.

God dreamed, created, and commissioned His church. He did not create the idea of the church; rather, He designed a leadership, guided it, and equipped its structure to mobilize the entire body of Christ, not just enabling and empowering the person speaking at the front. Why do you think God created the role of the prophet to lead and serve the church?

The true prophet is a person who hears God on a governmental level. It is the person to stand in the gap with messages straight from the heart of God. A prophet is a person to communicate direction, implementation, encouragement, and correction. In His great wisdom and infinite attention to detail, God structured the prophetic office to be a role and function in the modern-day church.

I have heard many ministers say that prophets are no longer valid, or even needed, because we can all prophesy and hear from God. Their reasoning is, since the curtain was torn on the day Jesus died, creating access to the throne of God through personal intimacy and relationship with Him, there is no need for the prophet - a person to whom God reveals His secrets. I want to challenge the doctrine that personal access abolishes the need for a prophet's calling and voice. Yes, we all have access to God on a personal level, but this does not mean we do not need the office of the prophet in the church today.

In Ephesians 4, Jesus is described as rising victorious from the grave, conquering Satan's hold and authority. Paul wrote that Jesus first descended (into hell), and then ascended, and when He ascended, He gave gifts to men. The scripture goes on to list and describe the five major apostolic roles, the second of which is the office of the prophet.

Just because someone has a calling to be a prophet does not automatically grant him or her authority and influence in the local church and beyond. A prophet must be recognized by other apostolic leaders, and even commissioned by them. Those with a call to the role and or the office of the prophet must learn to walk in, develop, and grow in this calling. We all have to begin at our current level of maturity, experience, and service. Without this development, how is anyone going to grow and qualify for greater responsibility?

It is God who created the role of the prophet for the flourishing of the church. With this knowledge and instruction from Scripture, who are we to reject this office or operation in our churches because we have experienced poor displays of maturity, wisdom, and ministry in the lives of those who are less developed?

THE IDENTITY OF A PROPHET

In order to go deeper on the role of a prophet, we must explore the identity of a prophet. In society in general, an extremely common conversation starter is, "What do you do?" The general first stage of getting to know someone is finding out where they spend the majority of their time, and perhaps, in the process their passions. We find out their occupation, career, or area of study, and then move on in our relationship with them from there.

It is amazing that we are unconsciously ingrained as humanity to measure someone's worth by what they do with his or her time, instead of finding out who they are as an individual. We cannot determine someone's value by what that person does for work. In the same way, we cannot determine the value of the prophet by merely knowing what they do. The common thread of quick questioning does not allow for understanding the *whys* of the matter.

So, let us talk about *who* prophets are. Once we understand who they are and who we are in relation, *then* we can better understand what a prophet does. Understanding who a prophet is, is encapsulated in the reality of their sonship or daughterhood with the Father.

From this foundational place of intimate familial relationship with God, His intended purpose over each of us is revealed.

A prophet is not someone with a gift; it is someone with a relationship with the Father, Jesus, and the Holy Spirit. This person has a relationship with God that is so amazing that it invokes identity, trust, and intimacy, building the bridge across which God shares His dreams, secrets, revelations, insights, destinies, and mysteries.

In fact, we lose ourselves when we make what we do an identifying value. We are so much more than what we do. Much like the ocean is so much more vast underneath the surface of the waves, so we as people are so much vaster and complex under the surface of what we do. The real excitement is what is inside.

God seeks intimacy with us first and foremost. Our whole identity comes from a place of intimacy with Him. Everything outside of intimacy is an act or a facade of what we do rather than who we are in Him. We will be hindered only if we refuse to be intimate and vulnerable with Him.

The most beautiful and valuable moments in my life are not found in great prophetic words I have spoken or in moments of extremely accurate discernment, or even when I have had angels standing in front of me. The pinnacle of my life's greatest moments has been when all the world around me stood still as my Father whispered His love into my ear. These moments, when I give Him my attention and am found in His love, are what have been the most beautiful.

A prophet is someone so lost in God that he or she begins to bear His heartbeat, burning with what burns His passion. After all, God does nothing without first revealing it to the prophets (Amos 3:7). They must be closest to hear Him first.

The truth is that when you are lost in God's love, then you will find your true identity.

The world has been designed to dismantle value, intimacy, and true identity from every single human born on this planet from the moment we were conceived. Even with all of the adversity we may have faced in our lives, all of the negative criticism, the horrible name-calling, the abuse, the disadvantages, the failures, and the lack of affirmation we may have experienced—one whisper from the mouth of God is all we need to breathe in real identity and worth. Purpose and security are found only in Him.

It is from this place, being filled up with His love, that we can carry out the role of being a prophet. But we must remember that it is never what we do but always who we are in Christ that determines our value and worth.

Too many people avoid quality intimacy with God. This becomes evident as these people put emphasis on being recognized for all they do and the power of their gifts, because intimacy has not given them identity. They grapple for recognition because they do not feel recognized by God in the secret place, and therefore they need that recognition from people on the outside. We must remember that Jesus explicitly warned us about this:

> *"Many will say to me in that day, 'Lord, Lord, have we not prophesied in Your name, cast out demons in Your name, and done many wonders in Your name?' And then I will*

declare to them, 'I never knew you; depart from Me, you who practice lawlessness!'" (Matthew 7:22–23).

Do you notice that Jesus values relationship above all performance? First, grasp this fact so you understand God's value system and what is of primary importance to Him. God does not care about what you do; He does, however, care about who you are with Him. He cares about intimacy with you, about who you are as an individual, and about the type of relationship you have with Him.

Remember Jesus said this: "For where your treasure is, there your heart will be also" (Matthew 6:21). If God has your heart, then everything else will be balanced and grounded in His love. We have been designed to serve and function in our destiny as a response to our time spent with our Father God. There are people who are so wounded that they are afraid of being intimate with God.But it is a dangerous path to continue functioning in a gift while refusing to be intimate with the source of that gift. Past hurt is not a reason for avoiding being intimate.

Intimacy with God and the work you put into that intimacy, is the well that is built by digging and placing walls of access straight to the stream itself. However, I urge you to pause right here and reflect on your heart for a moment. Do you flow out of private times with God, or are you just discerning or picking up from what is in the spiritual atmosphere? If you can honestly say to yourself that you are moving out of a private connection with God, His voice and His ways, then that is excellent. If you cannot say that is the case, then you may want to return to your first love. Do not let the applause of others act as a substitute for intimate partnership with God.

RECOGNIZED BY INTIMACY

Jesus did not need to be recognized by His title while ministering among people and His disciples here on earth. He even told His disciples not to tell anyone who He really was until the appointed time (Matthew 16:20). The Father recognized Jesus in the most public way when John baptized Him in the Jordan river (Matthew 3:13–17). But Jesus's personal identity was not in people's recognition of His gifts or His kingship. He humbly served those who would, for the most part, ultimately betray, abandon, and kill Him. And all this was in order to fulfill His call, which was the Father's will.

Jesus's secret was found in His lifestyle, of which we catch glimpses of in the Gospels. Mark writes, "Now in the morning, having risen a long while before daylight, He went out and departed to a solitary place; and there he prayed" (Mark 1:35). Jesus cultivated a secret time with the Father that fueled and directed everything He did. Remember a performer would have stopped at Gethsemane when all the applause fell silent, but it took a Son to submit to the cross.

Jesus's identity was fueled out of this intimacy, all He did He did from a place of being grounded in the Father's love, company, and presence. This is why He said, "Most assuredly, I say to you, the Son can do nothing of Himself, but what He sees the Father do;

for whatever He does, the Son also does in like manner" (John 5:19). A prophet who is truly intimate with God will walk and minister representing God's heart to the world. He or she will love with His love, and people will see the heart of the Father through that person.

Our primary role, as prophets, must always be to represent the Father to the world. Bringing a message from God into the world with His character absent in us will only harm people and the kingdom.

Defining a prophet in today's world is not as simple as it may seem. Those who care to know often find themselves asking, "What is a prophet?" The most common conclusion is that a prophet is someone who speaks words of knowledge and wisdom from the Spirit of God. This is true, but at the same time it is such a limited acknowledgement of the role and the gift that a prophet is to the church community.

It is never what we do or possess that dictates our identity or worth; rather, it is who we are as a son or a daughter of Father God that causes our worth and identity to be rooted and grounded. This only results from an intimate relationship with Him, not just knowledge of who we are and how God created us to function. The same is true for any son or daughter of God, no matter their calling.

In ancient medieval times, knights would ride their horses out onto the battlefields in full array, wearing their metal armor, going into combat with the enemy. Warriors would lead their armies and strengthen those following them with strong presentation and appearance. Simply wearing the metal armor did not make them a knight. It was the intimate knowledge, skills, and experience of combat and tactics, along with the use of weaponry, that authenticated them as knights. The identity of a knight was not in what they wore, although that made them look like one, but rather in who they were inside—the fortitude, experience, and the skill sets they possessed.

Often, people like to wear the armor—to have a title or appearance of a position of prophet—but the real identity of a prophet is not in a title, in the way that person talks or acts, or in a position. It is in who that person is spiritually, who he or she is with God intimately when no one is watching, and how mature and developed that person is in his or her walk with God in the area of the prophetic.

A prophet should never make gifting his or her identity. The prophet's ability to perform gifts is never a validation of the person, it is merely a fruit on the branches of the prophet's life. Just like an untrained person in a suit of armor is not a knight without first having proper training, so a prophet without proper training is just a person using a gift and a title. Identity can never be derived from what we do; identity is only found in who we are.

Rejection is a huge obstacle in people's lives that causes them to get identity and intimacy mixed up and backward. If people have deep-seeded roots of rejection and are not prepared to deal with them, then they will most likely look for affirmation and validation by overcompensating the value they place on gifts. Often, these people will look for affirmation, validation, and identity in the way they perform their gifts in the eyes of others. This is a parasitic condition in which the person flatters or wows people using his or her prophetic gift and then eagerly awaits applause in return. This is a codependent mentality that is excessively unhealthy and dangerous.

A fruit tree provides the best model to follow. A tree that is well planted, rooted, and established will flourish and produce fruit naturally, without effort or straining. Trees do not need fruit to prove that they are in fact a certain kind or type of tree. The fruit only confirms the type of tree. So, as prophets, we must first be grounded and rooted in God's heart as sons and daughters, for it is from this place that we are secured and established in who we are. Our spiritual fruit will naturally appear on the branches of our lives without force, confirming that we are in fact prophets.

A prophet will often have to speak or step into situations that are awkward, difficult, confrontational, and sometimes combative. If you plan on being a prophet and stepping into these situations as God leads you, then you must prepare for these moments. You must allow the weak areas of your life to be strengthened by God, so you are not easily attacked by the enemy due to missing pieces of spiritual armor.

For instance, there have been times when I have been prompted by the Lord to step into a particular situation. In these situations, I had to be confident that God was with me and for me. I had to be healed in my heart of rejection, fear of man, and insecurity. I had to know God's voice extremely well so that I did not just play a guessing game and hurt a lot of people and make a huge mess.

All of these areas of potential weaknesses are essential to mention, because a real prophet will be required to speak to people who are not going to want to hear it, definitely will not agree with it, and may likely begin to attack, slander, defame, or accuse him or her. In these moments, you must be 100 percent confident, secure, and healed in your heart. If you are not healed and whole, then you may begin to respond in an inappropriate way that begins to disqualify what you have said.

Convicted people are always looking to dismiss a truth that has cornered them, and if they cannot dismiss the truth, then they will attempt to disqualify or slander the messenger. So, this needs to be understood so that you are not surprised or wounded when it happens— that is, of course, if you intend on being an authentic prophet.

CHAPTER 2

BREAKING PROPHETIC STIGMAS, PART 1

Why is the prophetic office viewed as strange and untrusted in so many Christian circles and denominations today? An equally important question is, how should we actually view this ministry and role clearly through God's original intent? Oftentimes, in order to define something, we need to see clearly what something is not. Looking at bad examples allows us to better understand the genuine. Let us look at four common stigmas people often have regarding the role of the prophet today. We will look at two in this chapter and the other two in the following chapter.

Stigmas are either misconceptions or bad experiential-based opinions that affect our ability to view things clearly. The prophetic has its share of stigmas. The misconceptions surrounding different aspects of the prophetic function have limited people's ability to receive from God through this amazing avenue. We will dismantle each one so we understand each misconception more clearly and adjust our mind-sets toward this much-needed role in our lives, the church, and the world, both as spectators and participators.

PROPHETS APPEAR STRANGE

Prophets are unique. More often than not, they are misunderstood and seem as if they are in-between worlds. The first stigma we must break is that prophets are strange and that we have the right to dismiss them because we do not like how they come across, what they say, or how they say it. Let me explain the prophet's perspective with an example from history.

In 1969, the spaceflight *Apollo 11* landed the first two humans on the surface of the moon. That was the first time in the history of humanity that anyone had set foot on a surface other than earth. Since the creation of Adam, and even in the life of Abram (Abraham), when God told him to look up at the stars, every person who ever gazed up at the moon had an imaginary idea of what it was like up there. That was it—it was just imagination. The day astronauts Neil Armstrong and Buzz Aldrin stepped out of their lunar module and onto the moon's surface, their personal perception of the moon was forever changed. Equally, in that same life-changing moment, they looked up and saw the earth, from a perspective that no other human had seen. From that day on, these two men lived with unique perspective of the world. They saw earth from the outside. The vast majority of us will only see from the standpoint of looking toward the moon, but very few can say they have seen from both directions.

In a similar way, prophets have an extremely unique perspective of the world and of people. They have God's perspective! This is often why they come across disconnected from others. As a prophet, once you have seen things from God's world, that insight puts regular life into a clearer filter. When you look at the world and culture, you can never see things like you used to.

Often, prophets carry God-placed burdens for the church inside their beings. Like no other role, the expression of this can often be easily misunderstood. We, as the body of Christ, must do a better job of understanding why prophets say what they say at times, rather than judging at a shallow surface level and completely missing the gift of guidance God is blessing us with.

For a prophet, it can often feel like an internal GPS is trying to reroute a ship. An inner building of tension is desperately trying to bring course correction to the not-so-obvious will of God. Mary K. Baxter, a woman I hold as a spiritual momma, had an experience that some find hard to believe. She was taken by Jesus in the Spirit to places in hell over a series of forty nights. Jesus asked Mary to write books and to tell the world that hell is real. As you can imagine, she was deeply horrified by what she saw and experienced—so much so that she mentioned being physically sick during the days between these visits.

When I was twenty-one, I had a similar encounter with Jesus. Some of what I experienced was exactly as Mary described. Her testimony resonates with me deeply. She is much older now than when she had those original encounters, but when asked about it, she gets a serious look on her face and intently tells people hell is real and that Jesus is kind and loving, but we must repent and be saved from a lost eternity.

Prophets encounter what gives permanent shifts in perspectives and priorities. Not everyone can understand that. I have had people tell me, "You're too intense." The reason they feel that I am too intense is because they have not seen what I have seen. Once you have encountered something, you cannot compromise the conviction of your experience and insight. So, this can make our mere presence uncomfortable to those who encounter us or our message.

Even the best and most seasoned of prophets can be misunderstood in the best of circumstances. One problem we have as a culture today is that our generation has been taught to sharply critique everything in our lives. As a modern culture, we have become a consumer culture, which has spilled over into the church. If it offends our ego, we reject it. We presume to know what is best for us, thinking we are protecting our hearts. It sounds good, but it really is a poisonous belief system.

In the world of fitness today, for example, someone will pay huge sums of money for a personal trainer to put them through all kinds of grueling workouts that push them to the edge and make them sore the next day. And they do it again the following day. We recognize this as positive input in our lives, although it does not feel good in the moment. A business mentor or coach comes alongside a young entrepreneur or business owner and coaches them. However, they do not sit around like a cheerleader and praise all the great things being done; rather, they find what is not being done right and begin to correct the practice and mindset of the apprentice. If listened to, that mentor will add great value to the entrepreneur.

In the same way, prophets are sent to come alongside the body of Christ. Their role does not always seem pleasant, but when we understand their purpose, and that it is us who benefits from it, then we have a much simpler time letting them lead us and be free among us. We allow them to grow and flow in who they are to be to the body. It is interesting that we welcome paid coaching from secular realms, but the moment a prophet brings a word that may be uncomfortable, but for our good and benefit, rebellion rises up in our hearts.

Many prophets have been given a hard time and have been rejected over bringing inconvenient truth to light. People, in the name of protecting "self" and knowing what is "best for myself", have been over confident in their own ability to judge a matter. They seem slow to understand or even give attention to a word being brought by a prophet, perhaps because they have felt the prophet was too intense or seemed off in another realm and weird. But they do not stop to understand and discern that perhaps what is being said is in fact God's message. They have just missed it!

We as the church can never be so assured in ourselves and established in our own pride and confidence that we are unwilling to hear and discern a message from a credible prophet. Especially when they are words that are not necessarily immediately easy to receive or are packaged in a way we would like to receive them.

The first stigma we must break is that prophets are strange or too far out there. We can now begin to see the framework that outlines prophets as operating out of an entirely different perspective than most Christians. This perspective gives them an X factor that is easily misunderstood, rejected, and missed to the detriment of the body of Christ and individuals in need of the operation of the prophet.

THE FOOLISH AND RECKLESS PROPHET

Foolishness is the second stigma to be broken. We need to take a serious look at how foolishness has hurt and damaged each one of us at some point in our lives. Of course, this has happened by the foolishness of others, but let us never forget that we also have been authors of foolish and reckless behavior that has brought about pain in others as well.

Immaturity is often to blame for foolishness, but it is not the only culprit. Recklessness can also be a result of hastiness and misplaced zeal, a rebellious and unsubmitted heart, or an unloving motive in the heart of the prophet. The culmination of foolishness and immaturity have brought about a bad reputation for the authentic role of the prophet in many church communities. It has caused the rejection and denial of access to the real prophet and prophetic gifting. This is not just a problem on the part of the prophets; it is also a discernment issue on the part of the body of Christ and its leaders.

We know that a young teacher can overzealously deliver a theory or experience as a doctrinal fact; we also know that a young pastor will make mistakes as he or she develops in caring for the people he or she serves. We understand and have grace for these bumps in the road along the path to development, but we also need to learn to maturely manage the young and developing prophets in our communities. A healthy learning environment is a maturely stewarded atmosphere where we can safely make mistakes and learn from our errors in the pursuit of wiser operation of our gifts. But it's also a place where those around are testing the fruit and examining what is said with a little more scrutiny and understanding. Paul stated that when someone prophesies, the words should be judged by others:

> *"Let two or three prophets speak, and let the others judge. But if anything is revealed to another who sits by, let the first keep silent. For you can all prophesy one by one, that all may learn and all may be encouraged. And the spirits of the prophets are subject to the prophets. For God is not the author of confusion but of peace, as in all the churches of the saints" (1 Corinthians 14:29-33).*

You see, God loves to use His mouthpieces to deliver His heart, instruction, vision, and correction to our lives. However, we must remember that prophets are human beings who can make errors too. That is why Paul instructs us in this passage to "let the others judge." What does it mean, "others"? It simply means those who are listening to the prophecy.

We, as individuals, must judge what is being said over our lives. The Scriptures tell us to work out our own salvation with fear and trembling (Philippians 2:12). We are not to be naïve listeners or gullible onlookers following everything we hear. We are to be discerning assessors of what is said to us in the name of God.

I have seen, met, and heard of many people who just accept "prophecies" given to them without testing the words for authenticity, and face many hardships and troubles as a result of following something that was not God. There are two responsible parties here—the speakers and the hearers. The speaker is responsible for delivering a word that accurately communicates God's message and is responsible when the word is inaccurate or not from God. And equally, the hearers are responsible for what they have heard by either rejecting it or running with it without testing the word against God's Word and will.

Humans lean toward blaming others, in this case the prophet, for the wrong word instead of taking responsibility for not verifying with God that it was in fact Him and His Word. When someone says, "God is saying this or that," we must remember that it is our job as the hearers to test the message because messengers can sometimes get it wrong, especially young prophets who are still developing and growing in their gift.

We do not need to breed suspicion here; I am not talking about an intense sifting where we miss the joy of hearing God's voice through the prophet, but rather learning to deliver and be a helper to those who are delivering God's message. We are called to be one in the process of speaking and hearing. Each role is sacred and has responsibilities in itself for God's design for prophecy.

As prophets, it is our responsibility to become excellent and skilled in our role. Whether that is seeing into the visionary realm or hearing God's voice, it is about the delivery of relevant messages to God's people with God's heart. When we forget to walk humbly and with reverence of our role, ego grows and we become reckless and foolish in the way we behave and operate in our gifts. As a result of this, people naturally get hurt. We are responsible to develop and grow so we get this right.

We live in the natural world, but our awareness is heightened into the spiritual realm and reality too. Our job as prophets is to bring messages from the spiritual realm back into the natural world. And this is the reason why prophets have been given all kinds of names throughout the centuries, such as oracles, mystics, seers, harbingers, and heralders. Prophets have been recognized since the beginning of time. This is a weighty role and, as such, carries great responsibility and accountability to God.

The Word and the Spirit go together. I have seen many groups and individuals who have separated the aspects of the Spirit from the Word and become reckless operators of the prophetic with no balance, accountability, or wisdom. Over time, this recklessness has established entire movements and cultures that have not reflected the purity or purpose of God's original intent for this gift and office.

I love the charismatic and Pentecostal movements, but, as a whole, within these movements there can tend to be a lack of character and integrity. And to balance out that statement, we will find issues on the other side of this argument where movements and denominations have separated and discarded the Spirit and have only kept the Word, not recognizing that these two facets of God are one and can never be separated without a degenerated outcome.

When people only hold the Word without the illumination of Holy Spirit partnering and moving within the frame of the Word, they will mostly see a dry and ritualistic religion that lacks power. And movements that are out of balance holding mainly to the Spirit and minoring on the Word often find that people claim freedom and liberty to excuse their inherent rebellion to boundaries and requirements of the Word. This one-sidedness creates a polarizing ripple-effect that generally causes more damage than good.

After some time and consistency, people from either group will reject all of the revelation and freedom given to the other group. The Word-based group will have higher character and Word and will look down on the moves of the Spirit as foolish; and the Spirit-based groups will look down on the Word-based groups as too religious and regimented in discipline. Both will, however, reject the fullness of what God is doing in each group. The Spirit and the Word are married and should not be separated.

Many prophetic people have unfortunately established a reputation of being flakey, unsubmitted, and free spirits. And although there may be elements of prophetic skill, breakthrough, or even amazing revelation, there is no credibility because of the lack of character. Credibility is not what we do right, but more so what we do not do wrong.

Unfortunately, human nature is instinctively rebellious and fights what God does a lot of the time. So, we will often find reasons to discredit what we do not understand or are not familiar with. Often, it's not the gift that is criticized; it's the character flaws in the bearer of the gifts that seems to justify a person dismissing what is being done.

As a prophet, it's not just what we walk in prophetically that matters—it's how we walk in the prophetic and in our personal lives. We are called to live with integrity and character, and with humility, honor, and submission. Prophets and prophetic people need to rebuild credibility and bring healing to the body instead of disappointment and offense.

It is time for spiritual fathers to teach, activate, and properly disciple once again. In many circles, prophets have been stimulated with an awakened gift or awareness but never fathered into maturity. It is a breeding ground for recklessness and immaturity. Just look at any pack of wayward boys—they are not usually headed to the local library or to do community service. We see this same calling forth of gifts in courses, programs, and discipleship training schools but no fathering bringing those same gifts to maturity.

Fathers have only gone so far as teaching and activating the gifts of younger people in the faith. But this is nothing more than sending babies into the battlefield. Taking spiritual infants, who have just been "activated" or taught how to use one or more of their prophetic gifts, and commissioning them to go out and start ministering is one of the most foolish spiritual parenting concepts.

Not only is that young infant going to experience all kinds of issues, but you are empowering a person to potentially damage a large percentage of those who listen to the immature gifts in operation and then replicate the problem. I am not saying that people should not be activated in spiritual gifts and sent out into the community to reach the lost with words of knowledge and healing. What I am saying is that we cannot just call someone an officer of God without some serious training and testing first.

There was a great man of God in the early 1900s by the name of Smith Wigglesworth. This man saw the power of God move mightily in various forms throughout his ministry. On his deathbed, he prophesied a word we should all pay attention to: he said that there shall come a move of the Word, then there will come a move of the Spirit. Then there will come a move of the Word and the Spirit, and after that the end will come.

This prophetic statement not only reveals the plans and intentions of God, but also His wisdom. There is a definite reintroduction and expression of each of these two powerful facets of God's nature to us. But the ultimate goal is a marriage of these two veins in the church. Strength in the Word and strength in the Spirit leaves no room for recklessness and immaturity. Someone once said, "If you have the Spirit without the Word, you blow up. If you have the Word without the Spirit, you dry up. If you have both the Word and the Spirit, you grow up."

Foolish and reckless prophets have indeed given a poor name to the prophets. It is in growing up that we will break this stigma. We will break it by allowing God to raise up fathers in the faith to teach and correct us as prophets. We will break it by surrendering to God's Spirit and testing every word, as the hearer and as the speaker. And we will break this stigma by allowing maturity to come through the freedom of the Spirit and the grounding of the Word.

Being foolish and reckless in the prophetic is usually attributed to a lack of maturity and experience. Let us humble ourselves, grow in the fear of the Lord, learning that each person we minister to is a precious son or daughter of the King. We will then find haste is barely seen in our lives, thus breaking down years of hostility, and bringing healing and restoration of the role of the prophet in the body of Christ.

CHAPTER 3
_____

BREAKING PROPHETIC STIGMAS, PART 2

Stigmas are misconceptions that affect our ability to view something clearly. The prophetic has its share of stigmas. We looked at and dismantled two stigmas in the last chapter, and we will look at two more in this chapter and attempt to dismantle them. The misconceptions surrounding different aspects of the prophetic function have limited people's ability to receive from God. Hopefully we can understand each misconception more clearly and be able to better receive from God's mouthpieces.

WOMEN CAN'T BE PROPHETS

There are some people who believe that women should not be allowed to speak or minister in the church, let alone walk in the role of a prophet. As stigma three, let us discuss this and settle this foolish misconception. I have been amazed by the amount of people who have visited and belittled or disdained my wife ministering in our church because she is a woman. In my opinion and history of watching my wife, I have seen more integrity, character, and purity in both her spirit and anointing than many male ministers.

Without my wife's ministry, our church would not be balanced. She brings a facet and depth of God's nature into our community that I cannot replicate. For example, while I may be able to nurture our church members, my approach and delivery will never be the same as my wife's. While the body needs both male and female influences, God has designed that both men and women working in their fullness reveals a majestic part of Himself as a whole. When we stifle the female minister, we are withholding a part of God, just as stifling the male minister holds back a part of God. My wife is a valuable voice and jewel in our church community.

As seen in the book of Revelation, there is a rebuke to the church that tolerated Jezebel, who was a false prophetess. The church is not corrected for allowing a woman to minister; no, the church is corrected for tolerating a counterfeit in their midst. In no way was the church rebuked for facilitating a woman to stand in a position of the prophetic or it would have been made obvious by Jesus (Revelation 2:18–29).

Then there is the example of Priscilla and Aquilla, both wife and husband. Paul directly addresses and compliments these two. This was a powerful and dynamic husband-and-wife team that ministered on a high level. It is even rumored that Priscilla anonymously authored the book of Hebrews. Paul had so much respect for both Priscilla *and* Aquilla that he names them both on a few occasions. They both had notable value on a leadership level to the kingdom in the local church. If only male leadership and ministry mattered to God, then I am sure Paul would have only named the husband here.

If God is so opposed to women ministering, then why did he use Mary to carry, birth, and care for His own Son, Jesus? The role that Mary took was a maternal nurturing ministry role, which is akin to the pastoral role in today's church. She walked in the prophetic, stirring the hand of God to perform miracles, which we can clearly see at the wedding in Cana (John 2). It was here that Mary instigated Jesus, the Son of God, to turn a large quantity of water into wine. God saw it fit to use a woman, not a man, to reveal His Son on this unique level. This miracle was the start of His whole ministry.

The Word even goes as far as to memorialize Mary Magdalene who broke the alabaster jar over Jesus's feet and wiped His feet with her hair. Wherever the gospel is spoken, it will be told of what she did. It was perhaps the most intimate ministry Jesus received! And there are others like Deborah and Jael, whom God used in the Old Testament to defeat armies, kill generals, and act as prophets and lead the nation of Israel. God does not see women as lesser than men.

In the garden, He did not see Adam as whole until he had Eve. Both men and women are facets of God, because Adam was created from God, and God did not use new material for Eve—He used what He already created, the rib of Adam. God does not see Eve as lesser than Adam; He sees her as the puzzle piece He removed from

Adam. She was a reflection of Himself. Why would He call a part of Himself unfit for service?

When Jesus was accused of driving out demons by Beelzebub, He said that a kingdom divided against itself cannot stand. If God decided that women were not to minister, then He would be denying the power of His own reflection in women, which is ludicrous to think about. God telling a portion of Himself it's not allowed to be itself in fullness and fulfill that for which God sent it is like saying only men of a certain age or race can speak and minister because only they reflect God. Men and women are created in God's image, which is why God calls *both* men and women into positions to fulfill what He has called forth.

Let us turn our attention to the passage that all the "anti-women ministry" believers use to attempt to squash God's intent in the ability of daughters of the King to walk in His full design. Paul wrote:

> *"How is it then, brethren? Whenever you come together, each of you has a psalm, has a teaching, has a tongue, has a revelation, has an interpretation. Let all things be done for edification. If anyone speaks in a tongue, let there be two or at the most three, each in turn, and let one interpret. But if there is no interpreter, let him keep silent in church, and let him speak to himself and to God. Let two or three prophets speak, and let the others judge. But if anything is revealed to another who sits by, let the first keep silent. For you can all prophesy one by one, that all may learn and all may be encouraged. And the spirits of the prophets are subject to the prophets. For God is not the author of confusion but of peace, as in all the churches of the saints.*

Let your women keep silent in the churches, for they are not permitted to speak; but they are to be submissive, as the law also says. And if they want to learn something, let them ask their own husbands at home; for it is shameful for women to speak in church.

Or did the word of God come originally from you? Or was it you only that it reached? If anyone thinks himself to be a prophet or spiritual, let him acknowledge that the things which I write to you are the commandments of the Lord. But if anyone is ignorant, let him be ignorant.

Therefore, brethren, desire earnestly to prophesy, and do not forbid to speak with tongues. Let all things be done decently and in order" (1 Corinthians 14:26-40).

This passage has been used out of context to belittle and control women's involvement in the body of Christ for longer than any of us would like to admit. When we read one or two of these verses alone, isolated from the overall context and conversation, it can result in a different meaning from the original intent.

In 1 Corinthians 14, Paul is addressing the apparent disorder and elements of chaos that were happening in the early church of Corinth. At that time of writing, the church was new. Prior to salvation, there had only been Jewish synagogues —a Jewish system that completely separates men and women in worship and teaching - and a pagan culture known for its excess of perversion and sin. There was a pagan temple in Corinth with over a thousand female prostitutes servicing the city's men in ritual. It provided the women of that city a sense of leverage and power.

When the gospel entered Corinth, however, the women had to learn how to conduct themselves in fellowship. In fact, fellowship was a new concept, breaking down barriers between men and women, slave and free, and Jew and Gentile. This letter was written to the church at Corinth, which was a church that had many developmental issues that needed to be addressed as it formed. The church was thought to have a few members of Jewish origin, but the majority of members were made up of Gentiles who had been converted from paganism. There was a general element of the congregation that did not have a grid for how to behave in church fellowship.

In almost the entire chapter of 1 Corinthians 14, Paul was plainly laying out conduct and protocol expectations for the developing church. With this chaos and instruction in mind, let's look again at the key verses that are so misused by the modern church to silence women's voices in leadership roles and ministry:

> "Let your women keep silent in the churches, for they are not permitted to speak; but they are to be submissive, as the law also says. And if they want to learn something, let them ask their own husbands at home; for it is shameful for women to speak in church" (1 Corinthians 14:34–35).

This passage is not addressed to women ministering; rather, it's addressed to women in the congregation who should be listening to the message and not interrupting the flow of the services with outbursts. It's obvious that this passage was addressing a cultural issue, where it seemed like whenever anyone did not understand something being preached, they thought they could just burst out and ask a question and interrupt the preacher. Even though much has been written about this subject, my intent here is to touch on the stigma that has enabled the rejection of women as ministers based on a few scriptures that are taken out of context. This has caused many women to be silenced and the voice of God to be stifled.

To take this passage and forbid women from ministering in church is both foolish and naïve. If it was God's intent to forbid women from preaching, prophesying, praying, or worshiping, then why did Paul tell women in 1 Corinthians 11 to cover their heads when they prayed or prophesied? Clearly, the concept of restricting women from ministering has not come from God but from people bent on misinterpreting the Scriptures.

Ladies, God has called you to be an active part of the body of Christ. The rest of us need you to walk in your callings at the various capacities that you are ready to stand in. As long as everything is done out of intimacy with God and with humility, respectful decency, and order, you will find God's purpose in your life being revealed. The body of Christ needs women who walk humbly, boldly, and accurately in their destiny and callings.

PROPHETS ARE OPTIONAL

The modern church has gravitated to believe that prophets are optional, not by confession, but by action. Many believe from traditional practice that their local pastor is the all-encompassing counsel of God, and the church community does not need any other ministry. But this is a wrong belief and the fourth misconception we will seek to correct.

When Paul listed the roles of leadership in the church, he showed that God had a parental and leadership model for wholistic, healthy, nurturing, teaching, and guidance of the church. Looking at God's leadership plan, it is truly a glimpse into the amazing wisdom and brilliance of God's design. Paul writes in Ephesians:

> *"And He Himself gave some to be apostles, some prophets, some evangelists, and some pastors and teachers, for the equipping of the saints for the work of ministry, for the edifying of the body of Christ, till we all come to the unity of the faith and of the knowledge of the Son of God, to a perfect man, to the measure of the stature of the fullness of Christ; that we should no longer be children, tossed to and fro and carried about with every wind of doctrine, by the trickery of men, in the cunning craftiness of deceitful plotting, but, speaking the truth in love, may grow up in all things into Him who is the head—Christ—from whom the whole body, joined and knit together by what every joint supplies, according to the effective working by which every part does its share, causes growth of the body for the edifying of itself in love"* (Ephesians 4:11-16).

What does this passage tell us? It explains that God desires all of the body to grow and mature. It conveys that the church has been given five primary veins to bring about the ultimate goal of maturity and Christlikeness across the entire church body—not just a few individuals. It tells us that these leadership roles are gifts from God that are given for the benefit of the whole church. To dismiss or devalue any of these roles is an insult to God.

God understood humankind's tendency to polarize toward familiarity and comfort. If we look at the primary roles of the apostolic leadership team, we see a well-rounded full counsel of leadership. Unfortunately, when we look at the modern church, we primarily see pastors and teachers leading and a huge absence of prophets and apostles fulfilling the roles they were meant to fulfill. The Scriptures tell us:

> *"Preach the word! Be ready in season and out of season. Convince, rebuke, exhort, with all longsuffering and teaching. For the time will come when they will not endure sound doctrine, but according to their own desires, because they have itching ears, they will heap up for themselves teachers; and they will turn their ears away from the truth, and be turned aside to fables. But you be watchful in all things, endure afflictions, do the work of an evangelist, fulfill your ministry" (2 Timothy 4:2-5).*

In the fivefold leadership structure, there are two primary types of leadership: nurturing and building roles—evangelistic, pastoring, and teaching roles; and fathering and oversight roles—apostles and prophets. Each of these roles carries a slightly different nature and each administers varied values and qualities, but they are all equally important.

In today's church, we primarily see the nurturing roles leading the church, while the apostolic and father roles have been minimized. The reason that the apostolic and prophetic roles have been greatly minimized is because they are strong, decisive, and, at times, confrontational roles and voices to the church. The truth is that people don't like the "sound doctrine" or "truth" that these roles will often challenge us to return and adhere to. Our culture will label these attributes as control rather than what they are - the healthy submission to God's ways.

As it is, people will often find reasons to critique and find fault in leaders so they can shrug off the standards those leaders or prophets represent. Prophets have consistently been rejected and disposed of from the beginning of biblical history. A confrontational Word of the Lord to God's people often cost them their reputation or their lives. Jesus even wept over Jerusalem and said, "O Jerusalem, Jerusalem, the one who kills the prophets and stones those who are sent to her! How often I wanted to gather your children together, as a hen gathers her chicks under her wings, but you were not willing!" (Matthew 23:37).

The stigma here we must dispel and settle within ourselves is that prophets are not optional, nor are they disposable in the church. Yes, there can be bad examples of prophets operating in error and mistakes, but, as mentioned, this is true of all the apostolic gifts. We must regain a godly respect for those He chooses to send to us at times as messengers. It is our responsibility to recognize and respect those who minister to each of us and in our communities. Paul wrote:

> "And we urge you, brethren, to recognize those who labor among you, and are over you in the Lord and admonish you, and to esteem them very highly in love for their work's sake. Be at peace among yourselves. Now we exhort you, brethren, warn those who are unruly, comfort the fainthearted, uphold the weak, be patient with all. See that no one renders evil

*for evil to anyone, but always pursue what is good both for
yourselves and for all" (1 Thessalonians 5: 12-15).*

The content of Scriptures like this shake me when I examine the
core belief principles, relational structure, and pastoral leadership
of the modern church. Words like *warn, admonish, rebuke, correct,*
and *confront* are all threatening words to many leaders and church
attendees. We do not want people to leave our churches or our
meetings, unfollow us on social media, or discontinue supporting our
ministries because of an abrasively accurate and needed statement of
truth that could save a soul or avoid damage of destinies. We cannot
afford to become pleasers of people rather than pleasers of God.

Truth must be spoken in love, no matter the cost, or we have
reduced ourselves to be enablers of wayward people. They call
themselves children of God but are actually rebels who do not
endure sound teaching that will shape Christ inside of them. Real
prophets are often rejected for this straight talk, because people do
not like confrontation. Paul said, "Have I therefore become your
enemy because I tell you the truth?" (Galatians 4:16). A rebuke has
become an insult rather than something that brings safety. Rebuke
has always carried a bit of an insult, but today's society has so
drastically degraded proper respect that what was once heard, due
to a vessel speaking, is now mocked and disregarded. So today, we
do not stone prophets with literal stones—we unfollow them on
social media, and we do not give them platforms to speak in our
lives and communities anymore.

Like Jezebel in the Old Testament, we build a community of control and passive aggression. We only allow prophets to speak if they have an encouraging word of knowledge, and we make the valuable and yet sometimes inconvenient truth in their mouths optional and disposable. That is, if we are to let a true prophet speak at all. Even the Scriptures say that in the last days people will gather themselves teachers to tickle their ears rather than endure sound teaching. And this is one of the reasons that prophets who confront are becoming rare today. There is a rise of prophets who want to give flattering, overly positive, fortune-cookie type prophecies.

Prophets are not disposable to the church, but are essential and mandatory according to God's leadership design. As prophets, we must walk with all fear and trembling to steward this great honor to God and care for the people entrusted to us.

CONCLUSION

Prophets have a lot to face up to. They have to overcome rejection due to a possible strange label given from the body that does not understand that prophets operate out of another realm. True prophets have to overcome the bad taste of reckless and immature prophets who have hurt God's people through various issues. Female prophets have to face thousands of years of oppression and open their mouths in obedience to God, not fearing the judgment of those less inclined to search the Scriptures for truth about God's role for women ministers. And finally, prophets have to overcome the stigma that tells them they are optional in the body of Christ, facing off with the Pharaohs of this generation, who say, "You can say this much and no more." No, God is breaking the stigmas and releasing the mouths of His messengers, His friends, the prophets.

When it comes to prophetic misconceptions and stigmas, do not go along with popular ideas and teachings. Go first to the Scriptures and study a topic when it arises in church culture and examine what the Scriptures say to verify for yourself what is truth and what is just levels of cultural or popular superstition. Find out what is scripturally accurate.

Not all stigmas are legitimate—many are a result of someone's bad one-time experience. Be wise and walk in maturity and open your eyes to areas of prejudice. Decide today, as a prophet or as a member of body of Christ, to search out the truth of a matter and not be moved out of a reactionary hastiness and naivety.

It would be completely foolish to look at someone who is several hundred pounds heavier than you and decide that, because they abused food and ate without control, you should reject all food and never eat again. That would be ridiculous and ultimately put you into critical care at your local hospital. Likewise, extreme prejudice based on stigmas can look just as foolish when we do not ground our beliefs in the Word of God and in His spiritual leading.

CHAPTER 4

THE CHARACTERISTICS OF A PROPHET

You are you on purpose. God designed you for a specific task that does not look like most other people's. Prophets can often see the world in a completely different light than how others see it. But this different perspective is often extremely disconnected from mainstream thought. You may find this true of your own self or in the prophets you know and interact with. Prophets can sometimes feel displaced because of their odd or unique personalities.

While there are quite a few specific personality characteristics that are unique to prophets, let us take a look at just a few personality traits you may recognize that may help you understand yourself better.

A DEFENDER OF THE LAND

When I was twenty-four years old, I had just been getting to know the Holy Spirit for a couple of years. I was driving around town one day, and I heard His voice repeat a statement. I recognized the statement but did not clearly recognize the meaning in the moment. God began to repeat, "You are a satrap," over and over again. I recognized the word *satrap*, but in the moment, the meaning was not clear. Later that night, I remembered why I recognized the word—it was the title given to Daniel in Babylon. The title referred to a ruler who was a defender of the land. As it happened, Daniel was a prophet whose gifting qualified him to be an overseer and defender of the land under a pagan king.

Satrap describes the role and office of a prophet. As a prophet, you are a spokesperson and defender of the interests of our Father's kingdom. A prophet's role is not to play God on a power and ego trip with people. Please, work on your walk with God so that your gift is never a vehicle you use to gather validation and attention. Do the work and let your gift be a vehicle of service for others. God has clearly shown me what He made me to do and how that role works in the local church and beyond.

A prophet is not a feel-good fortune-teller, although we are used by God to speak encouraging words of hope and destiny into people's lives; we are so much more than that. Prophets are defenders and watchers of their given lands and territories, whether that be their households, communities, churches, cities, nations, or even globally—depending on their ranking or level of promotion in their office.

A prophet's function inside of the church is highly important to the health and well-being of the local church. There is a weighty responsibility on a prophet to protect, defend, and nurture his or her local church with the prophetic. (I am referring to a prophet who is recognized and empowered by his or her local church leadership.) A prophet cannot just setup a soapbox and assume leadership, spiritual dictatorship, or, equally worse, what I refer to as a "parking-lot ministry."

Parking-lot ministry is when someone who is not well-known to leadership starts to have private meetings outside of church in the parking lot or at homes to privately prophesy over people. The pastor would never approve of this happening. The pastor is divinely set over the church body to protect them from wolves, and I have seen people set up themselves as personal prophets, without placement from the pastoral leadership, seducing church members with "words from God" that are in fact false.

Every prophet must be submitted in all humility to the local church body leadership or the pastor of any church that prophet visits. Furthermore, his or her prophecies must be tested by the Word of God and the voice of two or three witnesses. There are too many lone-ranger prophets out there who are proud rogues with self-appointed opinions, with "thus saith the Lord" or "God is saying" in front of every statement they make.

Sometimes, when defining the function of prophet in a church, we must first outline what a prophet is not. I had to sit under a controlling young pastor for a few years, working hard to remain in obedience in the place God had me during that time. The young pastor was dysfunctional; however, because of God's order, I could not simply speak the Word of the Lord freely to address the areas hindering the presence of the Lord or the maturing of God's people. God had allowed this young pastor to sit in that position, and I had an obligation to submit to his God-ordained authority. That godly submission is respectful both to the Lord and to people in authority.

The Word of God says that we are not to cast our pearls before swine (Matthew 7:6). Sometimes, it is not wise to speak out what we see, as we may be trampled to pieces, and not because God allows us to "suffer for righteousness' sake," but because we may speak what we were not released to say. In that season, even though my prophetic gift was matured and accurate it was shut up because it was not empowered. I sat silent on many occasions because I was not given liberty to stand in my office, and I was quite happy and content to walk through that. In fact, it developed my character.

When God released me into my call on a greater level, my prophetic voice had more liberty to speak out at appropriate times when the Spirit was speaking. This is because God could trust me to hold my tongue until His cue, His direction, and His timing. It was this training in wisdom that held me. If I could counsel you to pursue something paramount to the development of your prophetic gift, I would advise you to pursue wisdom. It does not matter how great a prophetic word or revelation you have—if you do not have wisdom, you risk sabotaging the delivery and reception of any given word.

If the local church is a ship, then it is helpful to think of a prophet like the GPS. The prophet advises routes, he or she advises of problems ahead, and he or she foretells crucial information about where the church is going. The prophet also alarms and reroutes the navigation when the ship gets off course. A prophet is not the overall authority; he or she is only a voice. And depending on the level of service and leadership you stand in, the Holy Spirit will show you just how much input you are to offer, if any at all. You may be discerning some of these directions now, but if you are not in leadership or not invited to share your insight from God, then do not share what God has shown you. Stay patient and humble, recognizing that you are in a great season of opportunity to learn.

INTENSE SERIOUSNESS AND MISSION-TYPE FOCUS

Often, prophets can have a particular look of intense focus and seriousness in their eye. They can often see things as far more urgent or crucial than the rest of the world around them. This is my spiritual DNA expressing itself in my personality—I am a custom piece, designed for a purpose, and so are you. It is important that we understand our unique traits but not become so polarized that our focus is stuck in black holes of intensity, stress, and negativity.

The prophetic perspective can be such a vivid reality because of insight that it can be difficult to relate to those who cannot, or do not, see with the same perspective. When we do not give room for the reality of this fact—that others do not see as we do—it can be easy to become harsh and unloving toward people. And in doing so, we inflict great damage on others. When this harshness occurs, the people we are supposed to help, influence, and minister to can be wounded and find it hard to receive from us.

Most people in the body of Christ cannot relate to all the intensity that often comes from a prophet. Because of this, it becomes a skill; filtering how much intensity we allow those around us to see emanating from us. Above all, we need to remember to embrace the world through the filter of love.

Our intensity is important and has its place. I am not calling for prophets to be tame lions—not at all. Prophets are called to be watchmen on the walls. They are the soldiers who stand on the castle or city walls and scan the horizon for the enemy encroaching on the kingdom. Their purpose and position are an absolute requirement to the camp. In fact, not watching would leave room for attack and destruction of their city.

Because of the watchmen, everyone in the city is able to sleep, go about their lives, and relax within the city walls. They are ever-watching soldiers standing in high places on fortified walls and lookouts, watching both inside and outside the city walls for threats that might disrupt the peaceful conduct of the kingdom.

These soldiers are not casual or apathetic; they are intense. They have a role and a purpose to fulfill for all the people. They have a natural and developed heightened awareness of the threat of enemy activity, much more than many other roles in the kingdom. When they see enemy activity, they are not quiet or subdued. No, they are shouting, screaming, and ringing the warning alarm; calling everyone to action and attention.

The other side of this is we must remember to enjoy our lives as best as we can. God is the ultimate watchman, and sometimes we can get so caught up in our role that we forget it is God who has called us. He wants us to stand in our proper place doing what is required of us, but He does not want us to be intensely miserable or children who strive.

Let's look at Jesus Himself in the garden of Gethsemane, right before His hour arrived of extreme betrayal. Matthew writes:

> *"Then Jesus came with them to a place called Gethsemane, and said to the disciples, 'Sit here while I go and pray over there.' And He took with Him Peter and the two sons of Zebedee, and He began to be sorrowful and deeply distressed. Then He said to them, 'My soul is exceedingly sorrowful, even to death. Stay here and watch with Me.' He went a little farther and fell on His face, and prayed, saying, 'O My Father, if it is possible, let this cup pass from Me; nevertheless, not as I will, but as You will.'*
>
> *Then He came to the disciples and found them sleeping, and said to Peter, 'What! Could you not watch with Me one hour? Watch and pray, lest you enter into temptation. The spirit indeed is willing, but the flesh is weak.'"* (Matthew 26: 36-41).

Jesus clearly operated in intensity, focus, and seriousness on another level than the disciples. At times, you may find yourself operating within the same position. God might be calling you, putting some sort of burden on you or situation you are to pray through, while those closest to you seem to be taking spiritual naps right when you need their support! Remember not to be harsh with these people, because they do not yet understand what you are seeing from your place on the watchtower.

MISFITS

Have you ever felt disconnected to the general flow of society? Know that you are not alone. As a prophet, you might feel like a misfit or outcast and find yourself withdrawn from certain groups of people. A prophet's intensity and focus can cause him or her to feel disconnected, left out, and even lonely; not everyone appreciates the messages that are delivered by God when He uses you as a prophet.

This rejection you experience from others due to having to deliver inconvenient truths at times, or because you are simply holding to certain standards, often offends others. The reality is that most people do not like the truth—even truth that is spoken in love—and so they tend to have levels of passive aggressive distance from relationships. You cannot afford to take this personally. It is important to remember that people are not necessarily offended with you, but their offence is with God, the one from whom the message originated.

Likewise, prophets can feel disconnected based on the different value system and perspective they have in life. Recognition that you, as a prophet, see differently than others, and as a result might struggle to connect on more shallow topics and interests, is important. You cannot let feeling like you're on the outside or rejected or misunderstood move your heart to love less.

I had to deal with this reality in my younger years as a prophet. Rejection always invites us to reject in return, which is not the way of love. You are not a misfit, a reject, or a disconnected individual;

you are a valuable member of the family of God. People need you more than they often know. Likewise, you also need them more than you often recognize.

ON ALERT WHEN EVERYONE IS RELAXED

Prophets generally have a keen sense of future events, outcomes, and threats. Their senses are heightened to consequences that those who are not prophets are mostly oblivious to. This awareness can be gripping at times, sometimes to the extent that it's hard to focus on anything else. This prophetic sense, particularly the negative ones, can cause a prophet to appear disturbed and uneasy about what everyone else doesn't even seem to notice. Don't let this intensity worry or weary you. You may seem a little weird and crazy as times, but you are not crazy. God designed you differently on purpose.

The man in the lookout tower on the *Titanic* sounded a little crazy the minute he saw the iceberg in front of the ship's path. He probably went into a panic to warn everyone, yelling at the top of his lungs at anyone who could hear him. People down below decks in the ship's facilities—dining, dancing, and sleeping with no sense of what he was seeing—had a momentary calmness during the upper deck panic because they could not see what was happening, nor were they in a place to hear the warning.

You are not crazy. You are just exposed to seeing what other people do not see. You hear what other people do not hear, just like the *Titanic*'s crewman. It's perspective that gives insight. It's not crazy, in the correct manner, to take what God is showing you and go with it. Crazy would be the man in the lookout seeing the iceberg and staying quiet.

A SEER IS A VISUAL

Just like the *Titanic*'s crewman had a view of what was about to happen to the entire ship, so prophets see situations and events in a "future outcome timeline effect." That's where the term *seer* comes from. It's the unknown to come rather than an interpretation of what is, that differentiates the seer in the prophetic nature of God. It is a future glimpse rather than a present-tense. When I am being shown something by God, I can actually see it in my mind's eye. When I am seeing over other people's futures, I do not have a sense of knowing—I am actually watching a movie of what is taking place in my mind. My eyes are open, in a spiritual sense.

It has been my experience that most prophets are visual people. Meaning, you most likely learn best when you are looking at something rather than just having something described to you. In my businesses, I have huge whiteboards in both my offices because my ability to see the whole picture is how I achieve maximum productivity and planning. My prophetic seeing extends into all facets of how I productively function in my life. If you look, you will most likely see that you too have outlets of this type of seeing that help you to practically function in the real world.

One of the downsides (to the many upsides) of being a seer are the occasions when your eyes are open over others and you are exposed to their full pictures. Not all pictures are what you desire to see. It's important to quickly release unclean and demonic things you have seen. If the Lord has not called you to deal with that aspect, then you do not want to be hanging onto it like a snare in your own mind.

Sometimes we are made aware of unclean or demonic things, so we can deal with them and pray about them, and sometimes they are just revealed because our eyes are open to that realm. Just make sure that you are purifying your mind after ministering, just as you would wash your hands after physical labor. The mission is accomplished, and now you must wash off the debris.

SEEING IN ABSOLUTES

It's not hard to grasp that prophets tend to see in black-and-white absolutes. There is little, if any, room left for gray areas. The rest of the world does not see like this. The world likes to view life based on a scale, and everyone's scale is different. Prophets are not put together this way. Prophets see the world based solely on God's scale. They can easily be labeled bigots, judgmental, old-fashioned, and even unloving because everything is either black or white—there are no gray areas.

I like people who are direct and blunt with what they say. You never have to guess what they are thinking or if they are straddling a relational or political fence. I find a purity in the bluntness of an absolutely decided person. I think that is why in Revelation Jesus talks about the church in three different temperatures, clearly describing His view on right and wrong, committed and uncommitted:

> "And to the angel of the church of the Laodiceans write, 'These things says the Amen, the Faithful and True Witness, the Beginning of the creation of God: 'I know your works, that you are neither cold nor hot. I could wish you were cold or hot. So then, because you are lukewarm, and neither cold nor hot, I will vomit you out of My mouth.'" (Revelation 3: 14-16).

Jesus is not wasting His words in His address to the Laodicean church. If Jesus rolled up to many church communities speaking like this today, He would be deemed unloving and unkind. But here we clearly see the heart of God revealing the absolutes of black and white, right and wrong.

The truth is that we are not called to "water down" our decisiveness. God would take no pleasure in us softening the truth to be more accepted and relevant to the world or the church. You may feel like this trait inside of your personality is you being "too extreme," but it isn't. You are reflecting heaven's culture.

LOYAL TO THE DEATH

Undeveloped prophets can be loners, but the flip side to this statement is true prophets are in fact loyal to the death. There are three aspects I want to highlight around this loyalty trait in a prophet's personality.

Prophets are loyal to the truth, even at great costs. Prophets can get themselves in a lot of trouble at times by standing up for what is right. And we are not called to run from trouble, as long as it's in the right context and in the bounds of wisdom. Prophets hold an extremely high value on the truth, and a real prophet will be incredibly uncompromisingly loyal to this.

Many times, a prophet will be incredibly focused on discovering or uncovering the truth, and then he or she will be extremely loyal to hold that pillar authentically, in reality, and with integrity. I have watched many people compromise truth in the name of love and grace. But that is not love at all. True grace and mercy are only valid after we have walked through the realities of truth in love.

Prophets are loyal to projects and ventures they embark on. In most cases, once the scenario has been assessed and God has been inquired of on a matter, a prophet has an "all-in or nothing at all" mentality. He or she is carrying out the will of heaven. Prophets will become incredibly committed and focused to projects that they take on.

Prophets are loyal to people. If you are a prophet or have a prophet as a friend, then you will find them dependable and committed to the relationship. Loyalty and faithfulness are the traits of a true prophet. While prophets can struggle with loving people correctly from a pastoral perspective, a mature prophet will be loyal to people with the heart of the Father.

A PROPHET'S BASIC FUNCTIONS

Here are some more basic functions of a prophet.

Intimacy. The most important aspect any prophet can focus on is his or her personal intimacy with God. Otherwise, that prophet becomes a performer rather than a child of God who is functioning out of the overflow of relationship with Him.

Speak. A prophet is to speak and stand on the truth of what God is saying or has previously said, holding onto it personally and corporately. Often, it is not easy being a prophet, because you will sometimes deliver messages that people really do not want to hear.

Warn. Often, prophets will see danger or hazards far off and will be responsible to forewarn the right people so that precautions and adjustments can be made to steer away from any possible harm.

Navigation. Prophets have a responsibility to guide people toward God's plan and destiny. This guidance can be seen in declaring revelation concerning destiny and promises. But it can also be seen in bringing prophetic wisdom to people, so they can make the right decisions along the journey.

Correction. Prophets will often be used by God to confront and correct things in people or communities that are unhealthy, misguided, or just plain wrong. Without this standard, people do not see their error and will continue in conflict with God's perfect plan for their lives. This can be another difficult role, as often the prophet will be the minority bringing the truth. Prophets are preservers of the old paths of God, paths that should remain constant in our lives.

Encouragement. Prophets are not just correctors and bringers of rebuke; God has gifted prophets to bring much-needed encouragement and edifying input to lift the spirits of the people. People need encouragement on their journeys, and prophets need to remember this. People cannot handle or cope with a constant stream of intense input, correction, or future-telling prophecies; rather, they need lighter, soul-lifting encouragement. This may be in the form of a prophetic promise that keeps their focus on things ahead, or it may be an encouraging word of affirmation from the Father that person needed to hear in that moment. Encouragement straight from God via the prophet strengthens people's hearts and causes people to have perseverance.

Again, while these are not all the characteristics or a prophet, these are a few of the ways God has created those who are prophetically inclined. Recognize that you are not a misfit, but God created you the way you are for a purpose. That does not mean you use your God-given personality to trample on people, but rather to walk in love. But no matter the gifts God has given to you, there is a growing process that must be engaged in.

CHAPTER 5

THE PROPHETIC GROWING PROCESS

Gifts are given, but they are normally not given fully grown or mature or with the wisdom needed to operate in these gifts most effectively and to their full extent. Your gifting is not a reflection of how valuable or important you are to the entire body of Christ; it only reveals how God wants to use you for the benefit of the body. Time, good mentors, and learning from mistakes are the necessary ingredients to become more seasoned in your gifts.

Seasoned can be seen in two different ways: it can express seasoning or flavors added to bring about a full-bodied flavor, or it can be used to simply express the seasons of life taking their natural course. It is a well-established thought proposed by Malcolm Gladwell that to become truly great or to master any field of profession, skill, or craft, a person needs to invest about ten thousand hours of study.

One thing I have learned with the prophetic is practice is needed when learning how to operate in one's gifts and call. This practice requires a safe environment for the student to get it wrong and the space in humility to be able to get it wrong. Many zealous young prophets and prophetesses miss the space where failure is possible. They then send people on their way with a misleading word of the Lord and "God said" promises that are simply way off track and not accurate at all.

It's important to note that when receiving, sometimes people can have such a strong will in getting what they want with a particular word that they put pressure on the prophet with their expectations. In personal interactions, I will usually back away and not oblige their manic tension, or I will look into the Spirit and tell them what I see, even if I get nothing for the specific thing they are hoping to hear about.

I have learned in many cases it is better for people to hear God for themselves in certain areas. If I tell them what to do, they will hold me responsible if the going gets rough or if the delivered word does not turn out how they planned. If you do not teach people to hear God for themselves, you will by default cause them to become dependent on you for God's voice. As the prophet, you do not want to end up becoming everyone's fortune-teller. It is not God's plan for you, and it will not leave much room for you to live your life.

Jesus said "My sheep hear My voice" for a reason (see John 10:27). God wants all His children to be intimate with Him and to hear Him for themselves. Intimacy alleviates a lot of this desperate "I need the prophet to speak over me"–type approach. If you can hear God for the little everyday things in life, it opens up heavenly realms so that when a prophet does speak God's word over you, it can be that much more heaven based. If we can be faithful with the measure of gifting that God has given to us in the prophetic, if we will commit ourselves to stewarding intimacy, practicing in the capture and delivery of the word of the Lord, submitting to the prophetic mentor over us, then, in time, God will use us powerfully.

YOUR TRAINING

Being mentored and discipled has been the making of my life. If we want to become well-balanced, accurate, mature, and loving prophets who are authentically effective, then we must pursue being mentored and discipled by someone more mature in the faith than us.

I will always remember the day I met the man God used to disciple me in my early years in the prophetic. God will bring you around fathers or mothers to inherit years of wisdom, learning, and guidance from their lives.

When we are young prophets, God will align us with a mentor to train, equip, and guide us as we grow. If we try to listen to too many "mentoring voices" early on, we can become confused and conflicted. This slows our progress or can cause us to become rogues, thinking we do not need anyone to show us the way.

As time went on in my personal walk with God and in my journey as a prophet, I became more established and mature in the gift God was growing inside of me. When I began to transition into a more public ministry, I noticed God brought more fathers and mothers into my life. As a result, I have been enriched with multiple inputs and counsel in my role, and I have been able to minister with greater potency due to guidance from those further along the path than me.

I have been blessed to have more than one of these Elijah-and-Elisha relationships in which I have not just been taught, but I have been practically shown how to walk with God and in the aspects of the prophetic. Mentorship has steered me toward maturity in my gifting around the prophetic. The core of my growth is developed in my personal relationship with the Father, Son, and Holy Spirit, which is and always will be the foundation, but God also uses men or women to mentor and fashion a student.

God uses mentors like tools to sculpt the disciple. The mentor is not perfect, but neither is any student. The word *disciple* comes from "to discipline" or "to train." Be aware that the mentored student can sometimes resent the mentor if the heart condition of the student is not right. I have seen both great mentoring and fathering and also terrible examples of abuse in the name of mentoring. God calls us to be discerning but not critical. Honor is a crucial key in the pursuit of being mentored. I have the utmost respect for those who have poured into my life, even the ones who were not "perfect."

God promised to connect the hearts of earthly fathers with the hearts of the sons and the hearts of mothers with the daughters. One of the reasons for this is when hearts are connected, the anointing and generational blessings flow. I have experienced this anointing and blessing flow into my life. It had nothing to do with how academic I was, but everything to do with my heart being connected in right relationship - rightly submitted to the leadership and mentors positioned in my life. You see, submission to a healthy man or woman of God, who truly carries something in the Spirit, is not going to push you down; it actually boosts you up. This will place you onto their shoulders, to a place where their ceiling becomes your floor.

Having mentors in my life has been the safekeeping of my pathway and calling. They have kept me humble, directed me, assisted me in difficult and life-changing decisions, and offered me their wisdom and experience. They were and always will be further down the road of life than I am. In my experience, being mentored is not something that you grow out of or graduate from. These mentors have the right to speak into my life for the rest of my life. And I welcome their position.

Mentoring is not cheerleading; it's coaching. A mentor brings encouragement, advice, and correction, and even discipline, which is necessary, and we should expect them to. Degrees of interaction will vary based on the student's character, temperament, maturity, and humility. Be advised that no two relationships are the same, nor will they look the same. So never compare yourself with someone else.

Also, realize that God has your whole life set out in front of you. It's about the long-term plan. Do not let ambition for a name, ministry, or being well-known drive you into ministry success or maturity. Being able to prophesy is not your ticket into heaven or a job or recognition. Just being able to love like Jesus is a good sign that you are on the right track.

THE OFFICE OF THE PROPHET

THE IMPORTANCE OF BEING MENTORED

Let's take a look at the mentoring journey of Elisha the prophet:

> "So he departed from there, and found Elisha the son of Shaphat, who was plowing with twelve yoke of oxen before him, and he was with the twelfth. Then Elijah passed by him and threw his mantle on him. And he left the oxen and ran after Elijah, and said, 'Please let me kiss my father and my mother, and then I will follow you.'
>
> And he said to him, 'Go back again, for what have I done to you?'
>
> So Elisha turned back from him, and took a yoke of oxen and slaughtered them and boiled their flesh, using the oxen's equipment, and gave it to the people, and they ate. Then he arose and followed Elijah, and became his servant (1 Kings 19:19–21).

Elisha was already established and set up. He had to humble himself and detach from a *title* he thought he had, the *knowledge* he thought he had, the *value* he thought he had, the *security* he thought he had, to get a *mantle* he did not have. He did not get the mantle of Elijah when Elijah threw his cloak on him as he passed by; he got it ten years later after walking next to the man of God, being taught, corrected, trained, and anointed.

Elijah schooled Elisha for more than ten years. This goes against a lot of today's popular church culture. In today's culture, we see short-term courses labelled as discipleship courses. People go on a discipleship training program and think it will cause an impartation to take place. Today's church culture training structure looks more like a school or classroom rather than true discipleship.

The problem is we live in a generation that wants to get approved and promoted as fast as they possibly can. But the reality is that heaven's process takes significant time and is not just a fast pass. In order to succeed, you must be discipled, mentored, and schooled by a seasoned prophet. This mentorship is not just an association with a person of influence; it's an immersion of key people into your life. It's being fathered or mothered by someone who is mature beyond you. It's not just being mentored for the development of skills and gifting around the office of the prophet; mentorship benefits growth in all the areas of your life. For instance, the men I disciple are schooled on character, excellence, integrity, finances, relational stewardship, even down to small details like keeping their home or bedroom clean and tidy, dressing with excellence, and maintaining proper hygiene.

This may seem extreme to some; however, you can have the greatest word from God, but if you have not been trained how to present and carry yourself with excellence, who is going to take you seriously? Human nature is always looking for a reason to dismiss someone who is representing God's truth. So, the way we train to prepare ourselves is just as important as the gift we must learn to operate in.

Not preparing and training in these areas would be like painting a valuable painting over a piece of rotting canvas. Eventually, all the skill and effort that was invested into the artistic painting will be of no value, because the canvas that the art was expressed on was flawed, corrupted, or compromised and would eventually come to nothing. Everything would be wasted. Being an authentic disciple is one of the key ingredients in bringing success to your journey and office. You will find its value as a young and growing—and even mature—prophet.

Never quit listening to the instruction and advice from the person God uses to disciple you. There are always going to be things they can see that you cannot see. There is always going to be wisdom that you have yet to grasp. Although Esther had become queen and was successful, she always gave ear to her uncle Mordecai. Mordecai was the avenue God used to bring Esther the essential wisdom that ultimately saved her people.

We live in a generation of independence where people prefer to be discipled by peers and those barely ahead of them. How is that even wisdom? How can we think it an advantage to be fed by another who has barely more experience or maturity than we have? Jesus described this as the blind leading the blind. We cannot get more depth out of someone who has similar depth to us.

We live in a fatherless and independent generational culture. We prefer to have a peer affirm us rather than a father correct us and show us better ways. If this is causing levels of fear to rise in your heart, then you are the right person to be reading these words. You may have been hurt by father figures or leadership in the past, but you are going to have to rise up, pursue discipleship, and be healed along the journey. Missing out on authentic discipleship could impact and prevent your true calling from ever being realized the way God intended.

God perfectly foretold of our generation through the prophet Malachi in one of the final verses of the Old Testament -which reveals an important emphasis:

> *"Behold, I will send you Elijah the prophet before the coming of the great and dreadful day of the LORD. And he will turn the hearts of the fathers to the children, and the hearts of the children to their fathers, lest I come and strike the earth with a curse" (Malachi 4:5–6).*

The enemy is and has actively made war between generational relationships. When God blessed Abraham and made a covenant with him, it was a generational covenant. Later in generational history, God refers to Himself as the God of Abraham, Isaac, and Jacob. So, when God begins something, He is not just doing it for you or for one specific group of people, but for those who will come after you. God is constantly building a dream of generational legacy.

Here is His amazing strategy: each generation that obtains and passes along what they have received in God creates a platform out of the pinnacle of their progress for the coming generation. Their pinnacle becomes the floor of the next generation. The treasure and richness of God's wisdom and the momentum in God's kingdom progresses and is passed along with each generation. If this can be done, then the glory of God can cover the earth. Each coming generation could be saved all kinds of heartache and hard lessons simply by sitting at the feet of and being discipled by those who have walked the walk.

Your goal as a prophet is to be mentored and discipled by another prophet. There are things you need to learn from someone who is highly skilled and mature in the same area you want to grow in. What this means is, although other leaders may be great people, a teacher or an evangelist cannot authentically disciple you as a prophet. They may be able to mentor you in certain aspects of your faith, but they will not be able to help in the specific needs you have as a young prophet. They will never fully understand you or the unique training required to develop your gifts and calling.

My goal is that both my natural and spiritual sons progress further than I ever do. As their father and mentor, I know that in order for them to achieve that, they will need to live in the stance of disciples and not that of their independent contemporaries.

God will always take us from "glory to glory." This means that in the plan of God, He will always look to take us higher in our development and growth. Sometimes that process comes in a package or situation we do not want to accept. But I have learned that God is not as concerned with our comfort as He is with our development on the road to our destination.

Development has nothing to do with age. I have met young people who are wise and old people who are naive and foolish about prophetic roles. Development has everything to do with your willingness to learn, be instructed, be corrected, and be stretched. It's not just about a journey of making mistakes. But when we do make mistakes or get things wrong, we are humble enough to acknowledge them and learn from them, thus becoming wiser each time.

In many church circles, seniority seems to be dictated by age. I love the fact that when Jesus was just twelve years old, He was able to humbly teach and instruct the scribes and religious leaders in the temple (Luke 2:41–50). Jesus opened up the revelation of God's word to them. I am sure everyone marveled.

We see the apostle Paul encouraging his spiritual son Timothy, a protege in the faith, after what I am sure was many years into their fathering relationship: "Let no one despise your youth, but be an example to the believers ..." (1 Timothy 4:12). Paul did not place any emphasis on how old Timothy was; he placed emphasis on him confidently standing in his role as a discipled son.

In another instance, Paul said to the church that they were to receive Timothy as they would receive Paul. Because, as Paul went on to say, "I have no one else like minded except Timothy." In other words, Paul was saying that over time, the relationship fashioned the very same wisdom, beliefs, and principles in Timothy that Paul had learned and developed in his own ministry.

Timothy serving and being mentored will have caused another by-product of blessing, bypassing years of painful lessons that would have normally been learned from his own mistakes. Oh, I'm sure there were a few mistakes made, but as I've known mentorship to operate, Timothy learned many lessons from Paul's own testimony, teaching, and experiences, thus avoiding a lot of potholes in the road. This is what authentic discipleship and mentoring with the right father or mother should achieve in your life.

In our generation, many are looking for someone they can associate or affiliate with, and perhaps to even label them as a father or mother, without the true deep work of what one of these relationships ultimately yields if submitted to. You will never achieve as much regarding your calling and heavenly destiny if you attempt to bypass the crucial road of being discipled by a mentor, father, or mother.

Never be too big to be corrected or receive advice that can course correct your life or ministry for a more effective long-term result, even if you do not immediately understand some of the comments or direction. Fathers see details sons have not even considered yet, and mothers can sense aspects not grasped or even understood in the present. A mentor's value to your future almost has no way of being quantified. They will be able to see farther and with perspective into your present situations and future destinations. Seek out, honor, and learn to trust these gifts from God.

THE PROPHET'S PREPARATION PROCESS

If God has shown or told you that He is calling you to be a prophet, get ready, for you are about to embark on a great preparation process that may be far less than comfortable. God is a God of preparation. He prepared everyone He ever used, including His own Son Jesus.

Moses was prepared for eighty years—forty in Egypt and forty in the wilderness—to be used as God's mouthpiece and Israel's deliverer and leader. Elisha was schooled under Elijah for ten years prior to getting his mantle. David was in preparation for decades, from the time he was anointed to the time he sat on the throne. It was a journey that took him from fighting and killing Goliath, to serving and being persecuted and hunted by Saul, to living in caves, to being shown dishonor in place of honor, and through much more. And all this was in preparation for God's use. This list could be endless.

Often, God allows us to walk through seasons of adversity and hardship. And through it all, God shapes our character and faith. Most importantly, He is able to allow the negative and destructive strongholds in our character and makeup to come under pressure. This pressure causes us to have to address our issues and change. More often than not, this happens not so God can finally see the problems beneath the surface—He saw them all along—but rather so we can see the flaws in our makeup, repent of them, and partner with God to change.

God does not want us walking and operating in our own abilities, strength, human reasoning, or attempts of wisdom. His preparation process is meant for us to mature and obtain wisdom and to realize our absolute dependence on His voice, power, and ability to do anything for us and through us. He wants our total undoubting trust. And He wants you to walk worthy of your calling.

In most cases, God has a far different perspective than we do, particularly in relation to timing. John the Baptist stood in front of Herod and challenged Herod for taking his brother's wife. John the Baptist was the one Jesus asked to baptize him, which was in itself a prophetic act. You can trace the lineage of Aaron the high priest all the way down to John, who then essentially laid hands on Jesus and anointed Jesus to perform the high priest's duties at the cross. And yet John's ministry only spanned three months! Ninety-nine percent of his life was preparation, but the potency of those three months completely submitted to God will never be forgotten.

Many people sit back on their blessed assurance and wait for God to prepare the entire meal. This is simply not reality. God provides the ingredients, but He calls us to partner with Him in the process. The Word of God clearly says that the preparation of the heart is of the man, but the answer comes from the Lord.

Allow God's Word to have a solid foundation in your spirit and mind. On this you can then build the stone of principles, humility, character, integrity, maturity, wisdom, discipline, consistent relationship with Father God, Jesus, and the Holy Spirit. On this altar, you can place your old man—the old you, the flesh, your selfish will and desires—and sacrifice them, denying yourself and taking up your cross to follow Jesus. Put the sacrifice on top of the wood which speaks of the things you have had to cut down in your life, the idols and the strongholds.

There is a preparation of your own self that you will need to embark on. Foundations should be built with aspects that seem as simple as reading your Bible. How will you be able to discern if something you feel like God is showing or telling you lines up with the Word of God, if you are not well versed in biblical Scripture? Because if it does not, then you are potentially responsible for misleading people in the name of God. This is how most cults are started. Someone gets a "revelation," and twists a verse or two to validate a newfound slant on a doctrinal belief system, which is often just an excuse to do whatever they wanted anyway. They proceed to preach it and teach it to as many as will listen. If they or their audience are not well versed in Scripture, nor have hidden it in their hearts, how will they rightly divide the word of truth?

We must be grounded in the Word of God, which is one of our primary foundations as a child of God. It precedes any kind of calling, as it directly reflects our ability to relate to God, to know Him and begin to understand His ways. To be known as a friend of God is our primary goal before any kind of service. Most people look to titles and service for validation, worth and status, but this is completely wrong. We must focus on intimacy with Him.

If you allow this preparation process to be in the right order in your life, then you will enjoy your personal walk with God. This is much like my relationship with my wife. We first had a relationship and fell in love, then we got married and in time children came. Children, or fruit, are the result of love.

Do not try to be a prophet; rather, fall more in love with Jesus, Father God, and the Holy Spirit. Submit to, and take seriously, God's preparation of your heart and character, and things will begin to come together. You will naturally walk in your calling and role if you are diligent with what has been given to you.

YOUR PROGRESS WILL BE EVIDENT TO ALL

Paul wrote to Timothy:

> *"Let no one despise your youth, but be an example to the believers in word, in conduct, in love, in spirit, in faith, in purity. Till I come, give attention to reading, to exhortation, to doctrine. Do not neglect the gift that is in you, which was given to you by prophecy with the laying on of the hands of the eldership. Meditate on these things; give yourself entirely to them, that your progress may be evident to all. Take heed to yourself and to the doctrine. Continue in them, for in doing this you will save both yourself and those who hear you." (1 Timothy 4:12-16).*

The simple fact is that if you really are walking in humility and submission in deep intimacy with God, then your progress will become evident to all. And if you are being mentored, then the natural progression is for people to notice your progress and development. We are not to put our confidence or ego in people noticing our growth, but if people are going to receive from our ministry as a prophet, and if they are discerning, then they should be able to see our progress and development so they can trust the purity and maturity of our role.

Paul continues to instruct Timothy to completely devote himself to the prophetic vision and mandate over his call and equally the teaching of the Bible, so that he would be effective in the purpose of his call. This would both help his own soul and help him save people. This should also be a mandate for each us, as we continue to develop and walk out God's purpose and call over our lives.

CHAPTER 6

THE IMPORTANCE OF HAVING A HEALED HEART

Great ministers who make truly authentic impact on others are healed ministers. Pure prophets are healed prophets. The Bible places a huge emphasis on this point: "Above all else, guard your heart, for everything you do flows from it" (Proverbs 4:23).

Guarding our heart is not just how we deal with what is happening in the present moment; it's how we deal with past wounds and bruises that are still painful. You have surely felt a sting when a certain subject or person comes up in conversation, or ministry time, and a sharp edge comes out of the speaker's mouth. It's not pretty, is it? In fact, it's horrible.

That sharp, bitter, offensive, and unloving communication is not purely because the person woke up that morning and decided to be nasty. It came out of their mouth because of the state of their heart. Jesus reminds us, "A good man out of the good treasure of his heart brings forth good; and an evil man out of the evil treasure of his heart brings forth evil. For out of the abundance of the heart his mouth speaks" (Luke 6:45).

This certainly does not mean we isolate ourselves from people because junk comes out. If we did that, we would never fulfill our call or purpose as we disengage with community. We will never be able to create a safe space away from what could hurt us or be offensive toward us. Instead, we can create an inner place in our heart with God where we are not ensnared by internal or external hurts.

Jesus told us circumstances in life would be offensive: "Then He said to the disciples, 'It is impossible that no offenses should come, but woe to him through whom they do come!'" (Luke 17:1).

Too many sons and daughters of the King make the tragic circumstances they have experienced part of their identity. They say "I forgive" with their mouths, but their hearts are still bitter and hateful. We must learn forgiveness, or we will remain tainted in our hearts with bitterness and hatred. If we do not forgive, then all that comes out of our mouths will be flavored with our unhealed hearts. This is so important.

We will then not only carry unforgiveness and bitterness but also prejudice toward certain people or types of people. For instance, if you had a bad experience with an evangelist and never forgave him or her, then you will probably have an underlying prejudice toward the next evangelist you meet. This will likely cause you to miss, and even fight against, the perfect plan of God for your future.

It's tragic to encounter a person who has been hurt or wounded in life and has never gotten over the pain or walked through a healing process. They have become tainted, bitter, or just hardhearted. They walk, talk, and see everything through the filters of their wounds or past memories. Usually they are cynical, harsh in their assessments and judgements, and lack the capability to trust or believe the best.

We have all met these people. At times, we have been these people.

Take a step back for a moment and picture this person as a prophet. An unhealed heart in a prophet will result in wounds tainting what the prophet sees or hears. For instance, if a prophet has been betrayed and deeply hurt, and does not go to the Father and get healing in his or her heart, and walk through forgiveness, then he or she will begin to interpret things in the prophetic portal through the eyes of suspicion. This prophet will subconsciously project pain onto other people.

If we do not get rid of unforgiveness and pain, then we will not be walking in the fullness of the Father's love. We will, without meaning or intending to, begin to see people as possible threats to our lives or potential future betrayers.

There have been times in my life when I have known I was hurting over certain past issues. In these times, I purposely took a step back from actively flowing and ministering in the prophetic. It's not that I disengaged my gift from operating, but I prioritize my personal and spiritual well-being above any form of ministry. Knowing what is a priority is so important; in fact, it is the top priority.

When I am in a wounded state, I may deliver a tainted message. If you know you are jaded and not totally whole, it is wise to be cautious rather than bless someone with a prophetic word with flies in the ointment. I have been in the situation where someone who had done wrong to me, came into a position that required my prayer or prophecy over them. The challenge then becomes, am I going to rule from a soul realm or from a spirit realm? As a prophet, I have to put emotions aside, tap into the heavenly realm, and inquire of the Lord for their life. Ask any real prophet and they will tell you that this is a difficult thing to do at times. We have to deal with residual emotions even after we have walked through forgiveness and healing.

We are invited to speak exactly what is seen or heard over a person's life. Nothing added or taken away, because of our like or dislike toward that person. I heard a great statement early on in my walk in the prophetic: "One plus one is two; it is not three because you like the person. and it is not one because you dislike the person." We cannot add to dreams, visions, prophecies, or words God has told us because we really like a person. Doing that is playing God and is dangerous ground for any prophet, no matter how long that person has been in the prophetic.

I knew a man who was accurate in the prophetic, but there came a time in his life where, because he had not dealt with issues in his heart, he began to twist and contort prophetic words, dreams, and visions. He would use a dream or word and tell me what God had shown him involving me. Then I would hear the exact same dream being used on another person around him! The interpretation of it was given completely differently to the other person to achieve a different agenda over them.

This is nothing short of witchcraft, manipulation, and the Jezebel spirit. This is just a brief example of how twisted a prophet, who refuses to deal with a wounded heart, can become. Of course, there are many more extreme examples of ministerial manipulation; however, all of those instances start from an unguarded heart.

Always guard your heart, and never minister or flow out of a wounded or tainted filter. It's easy to stop identifying that in ministering to the church, you are serving Jesus and caring for His bride. It's too easy to shift from a serving consciousness to a mind-set of an ego wanting to be recognized or a gift needing to be noted by the masses. Strive to avoid this. Always be small in your own eyes and esteem, just like Jesus down on one knee washing His bride's feet.

You may have heard the well-known quote, "Wounded people wound people" or "hurt people hurt people." Think of an emotional wound like a doorway the devil can manipulate if it's left open or unhealed. It's like a knife stabbed in your side that did not get pulled out. Any time your enemy wants to weaken you, distract you, or cause you to back down, he will take a hold of that knife handle and twist it until you scream in pain and do what he wants. This is why we must not nurture wounds. God invites us to come to Him and be healed.

Jesus was wounded and bruised at the cross so we could be healed completely and free from the pain of wrongs in our past. The Word of God says, "Above all else, guard your heart, for from it flows the issues of life." This "above all" places an utmost importance on this principle for all Jesus-followers. So, before we set out on our ministry crusades to save the world, we must ensure we are pursuing healing and purity in our hearts as a huge priority in our lives.

It's not that we will not ever hurt. It's just that we need to start with what we have been harboring in our hearts and any area of soul wounds and pain. We give these areas to God our Father every day and ask Him to give us the will and the desire to forgive. This is a journey—a very important one.

I have had to walk through many of my own painful experiences over the years. I can not properly express to you the liberty I experience each time I work through heart issues with God and when I remember to guard my heart in a situation that previously would have caused a wound. It never works out to "just let it go." The truth is you have to surrender unforgiveness and hurt, and in the process exchange them for freedom. This is why the Bible says we are to turn the other cheek. When we realize that other people's treatment of us does not determine our value, we are able to release offences much easier. Jesus was murdered, and while being murdered, He begged God for their forgiveness. That's the kind of heart that God wants in us. He plainly says in Scripture that He takes our heart of stone, with all its hardness, hurts, opinions, and offences, and He gives us hearts of flesh, so we can feel again.

It's so important to understand that having a healed heart is not just crucial for the purity of the way we minister, but it's a safeguard against having missing sections of metaphorical armor. Unhealed wounds are entry points that can be taken advantage of by the enemy. Paul writes, "in order that Satan might not outwit us. For we are not unaware of his schemes" (2 Corinthians 2:11).

Once you accept this you will realize two things. First, you are incredibly valuable in God's plan and have a crucial part to play. Second, the enemy is actually more of a military type enemy rather than a little red man with a pitchfork. When the enemy schemes to attack you, he is doing so to remove or undermine your effectiveness, much like he did to Eve in the garden. He did not present himself as scary; he coerced her, using his intellect to woo her into making the choice to sin against God.

The enemy is crafty. He is not stupid. He never attacks your strong places. He always comes after the areas you are weak in or presume a weakness. Eve was lured because she did not believe she was really like God. She ate the fruit so that she could be like Him, not realizing that she was already created in the likeness of God.

Put simply, the enemy attacks the areas of your life he knows are wounded, or in which you are not yet victorious. A thief never enters a home when everyone is awake in the living room. He waits for a time when the residents are not there. Jesus said, "But understand this: If the owner of the house had known at what time of night the thief was coming, he would have kept watch and would not have let his house be broken into" (Matthew 24:43).

Guarding your heart is more than just being a person who ministers in purity and love. It's also about being a person who is protected from the snares and traps of the enemy that targets unhealed wounds. If the enemy cannot stop you from ministering, then he will encourage you to start before you are healed because that way you can do more damage than good.

A healed and protected heart is beautiful. As healing transpires and we take responsibility for guarding our hearts, we begin to take on the care, softness, and loving attributes of the Father. We minister as a reflection of His nature and less of our own. We will be able to say with John the Baptist: "He must increase, but I must decrease" (John 3:30).

John 3:30 describes my personal journey of looking less like Andrew Billings and more like Jesus. It's a lifelong journey. I am not who I used to be—I have so far to go—but I am a little more like Jesus than I was yesterday. Healing cleanses us of the toxic heart state that blocks us from reflecting Jesus in our personal lives and in the stewardship of the ministry He has given each one of us.

CHAPTER 7

THE ROBE
OF HUMILITY

Clothe yourself in humility, so that you never begin to worship your own gift. The prophetic gift and the office of a prophet can display some of the most extraordinary and amazing aspects of gifts and roles God assigns. The foretelling, truth-revealing accuracy and miraculous power of God that the prophet walks in can often be awe-inspiring to many who witness it. The wow factor can be significant and can be one that people at times will love and even begin to idolize.

As prophets, no matter how noticed our gift or anointing is, we must find ways to become less significant in our own eyes, avoiding people's need to attach significance to us. Jesus's approach to keeping His zealous young disciples grounded is important. When the seventy of them returned from a field trip of casting out devils and healing the sick they said that even the demons obeyed them. They felt a rush of supernatural authority and power for maybe the first time. Jesus response was, "Behold, I give you the authority to trample on serpents and scorpions, and over all the power of the enemy, and nothing shall by any means hurt you. Nevertheless do not rejoice in this, that the spirits are subject to you, but rather rejoice because your names are written in heaven" (Luke 10:19–20).

The power and authority Jesus's disciples were excited about is available to all of us as sons and daughters of God, but the principle of this instance applies well to those of us who walk in these amazing prophetic gifts and roles. Accurate prophetic words, visions, and dreams reveal astounding insight that shocks people at times with the detail and level of revelation. This will often cause people to treat you differently and place unhealthy levels of value on you. Attention and notoriety can be intoxicating and unhealthy if not handled with the right heart.

It takes humility to follow the Lord and speak what is not convenient or pleasant and will not get applause. But it takes an equal amount of humility to deliver words people want to hear! One of my greatest concerns when I look at this generation, is seeing prophets only operate in words of knowledge that flatter and excite people. This gift is for encouragement and love, but it can never be only that one dimensional. I love to bless my children with compliments and sweet foods, but they will soon become rebellious and sick if that is all I communicate and give them.

HUMILITY IS A STANCE

The sooner we realize that our gift is an envoy from God's throne entrusted into our lives to be used for His glory and not ours, the sooner we will understand our place. Not understanding this principle of humility will by default establish pride and ego in our hearts, just as it did in Lucifer's heart before he fell.

Lucifer used to lead worship before the throne of God, handling all the worship and glory that proceeded from heaven's citizens and was directed toward God who sat on the throne. Lucifer was like an administrator directing worship toward God, but over time he coveted that worship. Lucifer began to claim and receive some of the worship for himself. As this became established in his heart, he believed that it was his right and possession. And that's how the civil war happened in heaven. Sin was birthed in front of the most holy place in the universe.

The prophet is an administrative office that speaks on behalf of God and conveys what is being spoken at the throne toward people and specific situations. At times, the prophet will experience great majestic surges of power, flowing through and around him or her, as God speaks and acts via the gift bestowed on his or her life. The prophet may be tempted to become familiar and entitled to the gift that is in them. When this happens, the prophet is saying yes to the corruption and pollution of the purity of the delegated anointing God has entrusted them with.

Scripture instructs us "the fear of man is a snare" (Proverbs 29:25). If we are afraid of people's approval or disapproval more than God's, then we will become people pleasers and compromised in what we say. But we also know that the Word of God advises us "the fear of the LORD is the beginning of wisdom" (Proverbs 9:10). Having a healthy and reverential respect of God's awesome power and majesty will keep you on the right path of humility and cause you to not see yourself as great. Rather, worship the King and see Him as great. We are here to represent God, not act like we are Him. If God cannot trust us to speak difficult words and on difficult matters, what makes us think He will trust us with the easy matters where everyone loves what we have to say?

The prophet of God, specifically the prophet that is not for sale or corrupted by people's opinions, must at times enter into assignments from the Lord, understanding full well that he or she may come out the other side of the mission not looking great in other people's eyes. Real reputation and value must be measured by what the Father is speaking to you from the throne, not what people say or do not say.

How do we survive such difficult challenges and assignments? Survival is based on living a lifestyle of humility and brokenness before the Lord. Many people know how to present an appearance of humility, but real humility is measured in the heart, not by appearance. False humility is actually an ugly thing, where a person acts low, but, like Lucifer, internally craves and covets the praise, acceptance, and affirmation of others. We must ensure that we are genuine, and not acting a certain way to be recognized or affirmed for ministry purposes.

We must always remember that God assesses the motives and intents of our hearts, not our actions. Actions and spoken words are secondary in value to God. Words are simply not enough, because, after all, Judas Iscariot presented many words and actions to Jesus and the other disciples—so much so that he went unnoticed until his betrayal. Unfortunately, as time went on, something grew in his heart to betray Jesus for selfish gain—thirty pieces of silver to be exact. Judas's false humility let him be *within* the company of Jesus but not *of* it.

In our personal lives and public ministries, we must first be centered by our private ministry to the Lord. He has an amazing way of developing us in such a way that we live in reality and honesty. God is seeking sons and daughters who serve. He is looking for those who will, from a seated place of sonship and daughterhood, serve like bondservants.

In Scripture, those who were fulfilling the Great Commission started referring to themselves as bondservants as they grew in maturity in their ministry. Why did the ones Jesus called friends near the end of His time on earth seemingly revert to calling themselves bondservants after Jesus called them friends (John 15:15)?

Peter, Paul, Jude, James, and John all referred to themselves as bondservants (2 Peter 1:1; Titus 1:1; Jude 1; James 1:1; Revelation 1:1). If we look at the ministry of Paul, he referred to himself as the

THE OFFICE OF THE PROPHET

chief of the apostles, but as he went on in his ministry, maturing, he began to call himself a bondservant.

The term *bondservant* became widely used among the apostles because it created the perfect picture of us as Christ-followers. We can read in Exodus 21:5–6 the terms of a servant becoming a bondservant. When we decide to follow Jesus, He invites us home, and when we begin to taste and see that the Lord is so good, we cannot help but want to be joined to the Lord forever.

In ancient times, when a slave was set free from his time of service, he had two options: he could leave the master and start his own new life; or, out of love, he could decide to stay with his master, bonding himself to his master for life. If a slave chose the latter, it meant he was freely agreeing to stay with that master for the rest of his life. It is no wonder the apostles adopted this term. Once they saw how good God was, they never wanted to be parted from Him. This is an absolute picture of the willful and humble submission that each of the apostles came to in their walk with Jesus.

Pride seeks to build its own name, reputation, and ego. It wants numbers in meetings, fan clubs, and followings on social media and public forums. Pride does not genuinely care about the well-being and outcome of those it's ministering to, but rather that its personal "brand" and popularity grow into Christian celebrity status.

The modern church's progress looks more like loosened standards and saints leaving the narrow road of God, and lowering themselves, putting their faith in leaders rather than in God. We idolize Christian celebrities ... and the sad part of it is that many of the well-known ministers have mostly allowed this adoration. Instead of pointing people back to Jesus, they are creating a need for people they lead back to themselves as God's mouthpiece, rather than back to God Himself.

We survive when humility is the safeguard, the body armor, and the protection that causes us to maintain a low posture and walk below the poison arrows of self and self-promotion. When we truly understand just how awesome and magnificent God our Father is, it causes us to reposition ourselves in a place of humility. Each time we look at Him through the eyes of our hearts, it leads us back toward a stance of humility. This causes us to recognize a great big, perfect, loving, and holy God. We see His power and majesty, and, in the same moment, we recognize our need for Him in our lives. Our dependency is on Him in our every breath, word, action, and decision. From this place, how can we ever see ourselves as great? We capture the awe with which we are loved and made, which naturally brings humility into our hearts, without any effort or act.

I had the privilege of visiting Oral Roberts, a great man of faith, in his home with a friend a few months before he upgraded his residence to the streets of heaven. We asked him how he dealt with all of the publicity and notoriety of his life and ministry, and how he went the distance walking in integrity before the Lord. His answer was the advice he received from his mother way back when he first started his ministry as a single young man: "Always stay small in your own eyes, Oral." This statement deeply imprinted on me. If we are constantly beholding a great, awesome God, how can we ever see ourselves as the center?

We must always walk humbly before our God and remember that in all we do, in all we say, in everything that God has for us, He is the one who gets all the credit and glory. We are just a fortunate son or daughter who is privileged to carry His torch so the world can see Jesus, leading the church to remember their first love and stay the course.

We have a need for our God-given identity to be realized through consistent intimacy with the Lord. This causes us to never connect our identity, value, or worth to the way our spiritual gifts function and operate. It's easy to stop and ponder how great we really are after people begin to praise us for giving such accurate prophetic words, words of knowledge, having visitations from the heavenly realm, visions and dreams, and promises of greatness and destiny. However, we must train ourselves to be on alert. It's too easy to unknowingly allow pride to grow in our hearts. It takes root when we begin to take credit for the power or glory of God manifesting through and in our lives.

PRIDE WILL TAKE THE CREDIT

Of all the sins, pride is the most repulsive to God and the greatest blinder to the person caught in its trap. The Bible has a lot to say about pride and humility in Proverbs. For example, it says,

"Everyone proud in heart is an abomination to the LORD; though they join forces, none will go unpunished" (Proverbs 16:5).

Pride is so blinding that it causes many people to make terrible mistakes. It is too easy for people to overestimate themselves and underestimate outside factors and other people. People become infatuated with their own abilities and greatness, almost taking a posture of self-worship. This was the proposal that caused Eve to eat the fruit in the garden. The serpent did not speak to her humility; rather, he spoke to her curiosity for being like God. The devil never encourages authentic humility; after all, he is the embodiment of pride. After becoming confident in his own beauty and greatness, he thought he could revolt and overthrow his own creator.

Lucifer's story, like Eve's, did not achieve the outcome initially expected. This is because pride is an intoxicating elixir that ultimately deceives us into blindness while presenting a false reality. Both Eve and Lucifer believed the lie that God shares His glory with others and we can share in His Godliness. This has never been nor will ever be the case.

The Bible explains it like this: "Pride goes before destruction, and a haughty spirit before a fall. Better to be of a humble spirit with the lowly, than to divide the spoil with the proud" (Proverbs 16:18-19).

In World War I, soldiers often fought crouched in trenches. Trenches were dug-out positions that allowed them to stay out of the enemy's line of fire. They would carefully stand up to shoot, but had to duck back down to not risk being exposed and shot. Occasionally, a soldier would forget the danger and would become casual, stand up, and attract enemy fire.

Pride looks like this. We become so confident in our own abilities that, if we do not remain close and submitted to Jesus, we are easily tempted to forget our posture of humility. This false sense of confidence can deceive us into thinking that the rules or dangers do not apply to us, and we stand up and open ourselves up for attack from the enemy or even self-sabotage.

But the Bible reminds us: "God resists the proud, but gives grace to the humble" (James 4:6). If we want God to bless us and assist us, then humility is the only way. We do not want God's hand being held back from helping, blessing, and protecting us. We need to walk in humility. Perhaps James sums it up the best when he writes, "Humble yourselves in the sight of the Lord, and He will lift you up" (James 4:10).

CHAPTER 8

SPEAKING AS AN ORACLE OF GOD

When a prophet speaks a message that he or she believes is from God, the prophet is speaking while representing God. This is not done casually or timidly. We are not casual with God's messages, but rather we speak with boldness and confidence. If we are truly going to speak on God's behalf, then we must do so representing Him well, in both delivery and personal posture.

In this culture, many people in ministry lean toward copying the popular model or style of other ministries and ministers. Instead of developing their own unique delivery style or approach, people can tend to mimic and copy someone else's prophetic identity. This will often seem weird or strained when it does not come naturally. This is a shame, because their unique identity and style is lost while trying to be like someone else.

In so many instances, people appear prepared to dilute the potency of God's Word or what the Spirit truly wants to do or say to remain popular. Put simply, we know some prophets crave people's

THE OFFICE OF THE PROPHET

popularity rather than God's approval, and that is not something we can allow ourselves to do. It's easy to give exciting prophetic words to people, but the mark of a real prophet is not how many nice words he or she can give to others, it is how well he or she can deliver the words that are challenging or even unpleasant without watering down the original message. As a prophet, you are going to need to make a decision if you are going to be a Moses or an Aaron type.

After the children of Israel were delivered from slavery in Egypt and miraculously crossed the Red Sea and began their journey across the desert, they arrived at Sinai, where Moses hiked up the mountain to meet with God. There he received the tablets that God engraved His ten laws for the people. But while Moses was up on the mountain, Aaron, who was supposed to be the high priest representing God, conformed to the wishes of the people and constructed a giant golden calf for the people to worship. It was pagan temple–style event with all kinds of debauchery.

On one hand, Moses came down from the mountain and represented God's nature to the people. But on the other hand, Aaron represented the people's nature and culture to God. Will you be a conformist or represent what God is saying and hold up the standards of His will, no matter how bad you may sometimes look?

At times, especially when we are developing, the enemy will try to intimidate us in order to quench our boldness. It will often take a great deal of courage to get the message out of our mouths with the right level of presentation. We must rid ourselves of all timidity and represent the Father when we speak on His behalf. This can take some practice. We must learn to do this in our own personal flavor, without trying to clone someone else's presentation. God gave you the message to deliver for a reason.

I love the way God encouraged and called Jeremiah into his ministry. You can see God was speaking right into the core of this very subject in Jeremiah's heart at the onset of his journey as God's mouthpiece.

> *"Then the word of the Lord came to me, saying: 'Before I formed you in the womb I knew you; before you were born I sanctified you; I ordained you a prophet to the nations.'*
>
> *Then said I: 'Ah, Lord God! Behold, I cannot speak, for I am a youth.'*
>
> *But the Lord said to me: 'Do not say, 'I am a youth,' For you shall go to all to whom I send you, and whatever I command you, you shall speak. Do not be afraid of their faces, for I am with you to deliver you,' says the Lord.*
>
> *Then the Lord put forth His hand and touched my mouth, and the Lord said to me: 'Behold, I have put My words in your mouth. See, I have this day set you over the nations and over the kingdoms, to root out and to pull down, to destroy and to throw down, to build and to plant.'" (Jeremiah 1:4-10).*

It's both empowering and humbling when God lets you know He is with you and will back you up like He did with Jeremiah. God confirms that you are His chosen, and His affirmation and purpose is with you.

We can see this same affirmation of not only power but of words spoken describing the life of the prophet Samuel: "The Lord was with him and none of his words fall to the ground" (1 Samuel 3:19). This is true of all the authentic prophets, and it is also true of you in your life and ministry as you walk in purity with the Lord.

Once we have this confidence, we must always remember to walk humbly to keep things healthy and in balance. Once we understand this endorsement of God on our lives and learn the art of walking in courage and humility, we must begin to minister with grounded boldness with the focal purpose of building the kingdom. Peter coins this perfectly when he writes:

> *"As each one has received a gift, minister it to one another, as good stewards of the manifold grace of God. If anyone speaks, let him speak as the oracles of God. If anyone ministers, let him do it as with the ability which God supplies, that in all things God may be glorified through Jesus Christ, to whom belong the glory and the dominion forever and ever. Amen."* (1 Peter 4:10-11).

WEIGHTY WORDS

As a prophet, you need to be clear in your understanding of just how powerful your words can be. Of course, every person must be careful of what he or she says, because the tongue is such a powerful part of the body. But prophets have an additional emphasis here, as prophets are anointed to speak God's words, and with that comes additional spiritual power and responsibility.

I want to take a look at vivid examples of the specific anointing that prophets carry in their mouths. Mark 11:12–25 tells us that

Jesus walked past a fig tree on His way to minister. Even though it was not the season fig trees produce figs, Jesus still looked for figs on the tree. There were no figs, so Jesus cursed the fig tree. When Jesus and the disciples came back the following day, they found the fig tree dead. Jesus showed how powerful words are, so much so that He spoke and a tree died.

Another amazing instance is when Elisha was being mocked by children. Elijah had been taken up to heaven by a chariot and Elisha was left as his successor. Elisha was also bald. He had a powerful ministry and anointing, but he had some insecurities and an anger problem. Children started mocking Elisha. The Bible says:

> *"Then he went up from there to Bethel; and as he was going up the road, some youths came from the city and mocked him, and said to him, 'Go up, you baldhead! Go up, you baldhead!'*
>
> *So he turned around and looked at them, and pronounced a curse on them in the name of the LORD. And two female bears came out of the woods and mauled forty-two of the youths.*
>
> *Then he went from there to Mount Carmel, and from there he returned to Samaria"* (2 Kings 2:23–25).

In this instance, Elisha did not have much long-suffering as he called two female bears out of the woods and they killed the children. This is a sobering example of the abuse of prophetic power.

In another example, Moses was also powerfully backed by God as His spokesman. When he was sent back to Egypt to challenge Pharaoh to release the Israelites from four hundred years of slavery, we witness the powerful effect of God's power being released through Moses. We see this prophetic power when Moses was challenged by the sorcerers and witches in Pharaoh's court. Moses had Aaron throw his staff to the ground, and it turned into a snake. The sorcerers mimicked the feat, but then Moses's rod swallowed up the other snakes. Then God released the ten plagues smashing Egypt and crumbling Pharaoh's willpower.

Zacharias, Elizabeth's husband, was told by an angel about his son in the womb (Luke 1:5–25, 57–64). The child would be born of God and was to be called John. John would grow up to be another great prophet, John the Baptist. Zacharias was a priest who had no children. When his turn came to burn the incense in the temple, the angel Gabriel appeared to declare the coming of John the Baptist. Zacharias tried to reason with Gabriel that he was too old to preserve the word of the Lord until it's coming. Gabriel then struck Zacharias so he was unable to speak. If he had not spoken against God's plan, who knows how the story could have changed. He later got his voice back, and His son played a key role in the coming of the King.

These are powerful examples of both successful and unsuccessful operations of powerful entrusted authority in the tongue of believers, but particularly in the mouth of prophets.

There are times when we are so careless with our words, we become casual with the delegated creative power of our tongues. Proverbs 18:21 reminds us "death and life are in the power of the tongue." It's easy to become casual and familiar with the choice of words we use. We easily forget that the power held in our tongues can change the course of our lives and the lives of those around us. This change can be for better or worse, depending on the way we decide to speak.

If Jesus could curse a fig tree with His words and the tree died, then so can you. Jesus was not trying to put on a show; rather, He was trying to get a point across to all Christians that our mouths are powerful instruments that can create or destroy. Even though all people can create life and death with their tongues, a prophet seems to have more authority in this area and so must take extra caution to measure his or her words.

Someone who carries the prophetic mantle has the ability to bless or curse. Sometimes we can pronounce curses on people with our words because emotions take over or perhaps we have harbored unforgiveness and bitterness, and our words are tainted with everything opposite of love. But when the power to speak and create or destroy is mixed with the wrong heart, we are prone to operate in Christian witchcraft.

A prophet or prophetess needs to ensure that they are God's mouthpiece and not a mixture of God's will and the devil's will. The power of creative life in the mouth of the prophet, or a powerful declaration that assaults the kingdom of darkness, is the purpose of the authority we have been given.

LOOSE LIPS SINK SHIPS

The power of words is so often misunderstood and misused. There was a catchphrase in World War II that said "loose lips sink ships." This was a literal interpretation, it was not a metaphor. Behind closed doors, military intelligence, reconnaissance, and mission planning took place. The military and civilian personnel who were involved in these bases were privy to extremely sensitive and top-secret information and strategies. If any of these people leaked mail or even a hint of information outside trusted circles, a crucial piece of intelligence would be broken. Consequently, losses and damage would happen if that information got into enemy hands.

The phrase "loose lips sink ships" had serious consequences, as the Allies would know and plan the position and shipping routes of all supply convoys and war ships across the oceans of the earth. If their ships' positions were given away by careless conversation or a senseless intelligence officer shooting his mouth off, the penalty would be court marshaling and that person would account for every word and motive. In these wartime situations, there were always spies scattered listening for any information to report back. The secrets divulged were not safe because spies would take this information and deliver it to enemy command. Fleets of ships would be intercepted, causing serious loss of men, supplies, and ships.

We often forget, lose our inhibitions, wisdom, senses, and discretion when we fail to walk correctly in the Spirit and are drawn out by our fleshly nature and emotions. A child of God has the most powerful delegation of potency in their words. Life and death are in the tongue.

We are not always in a situation where we are privy to kingdom intelligence, but we all have the significant superpower of blessing and cursing with our words. This power can really affect people if misused. Name calling, hurtful statements and gossip are negatively powerful and destructive weapons that can, and do, cause great damage to people's lives.

John the Baptist's father was a high priest in the temple. He was struck speechless for more than just a sign. Because of who he was and the mantle he carried, until he had the revelation of who his son would be born to be, he was not able to speak or name the child, because his words carried great power. The Hebrew people understood far better than most do today the power of words, names and meanings, and blessing and cursing.

When the children of Israel were in front of the city of Jericho, a people who had a forty-year track record of murmuring and complaining, God's instructions to Joshua for the people were simple: walk and do not talk.

Joshua had the people silently walk around the city for six days, and then on the seventh day, at the end of the circuits they had to let out a great shout. What happened next was miraculous - the city walls collapsed. The power of words is so crucial that God ensured they did not speak a word in case they spoke death over what they were doing and defeated the purpose of the act.

I remember watching a cartoon with a little bunny rabbit who said, "If you can't say something nice, don't say anything at all." It stuck with me because it is a powerful creed to live by. Let us modify that just a fraction and say, "If you can't speak words of life, it's best not to speak at all." There is power in your mouth to bless people, but it is also there to tear down the enemy's kingdom.

Ephesians instructs us that our warfare is not against flesh and blood, but against spiritual demonic forces and powers (Ephesians 6:10–20). So, our enemy is not the person who hurt our feelings. It is our job to destroy the devil's kingdom and to love people, even if that is tough love at times. Train your mouth to only speak what God would have you say to the right person or situation at the right time.

When we speak, we are speaking as oracles of God: "As each one has received a gift, minister it to one another, as good stewards of the manifold grace of God. If anyone speaks, let him speak as the oracles of God. If anyone ministers, let him do it as with the ability which God supplies, that in all things God may be glorified through Jesus Christ, to whom belong the glory and the dominion forever and ever. Amen" (1 Peter 4:10–11).

CHAPTER 9

PROPHETIC CREATIVITY AND EXPRESSION

Prophets usually have a highly functioning imagination and visual perception. Perhaps it is not realized, but throughout history, and still today, prophetic people have been closely connected to the expression of creativity and advancement in the earth. Personally, I am an incredibly visual person. When someone shares a story or even a vision they have experienced, it's like I can see everything they are describing as they describe it to me.

Many times, people who are designed by God with prophetic tendencies shrug off their prophetic nature as personality traits, abilities, hobbies, or creative expression. Unless they are connected with Holy Ghost, they most likely do not realize that their personality is actually a tool for God to manifest His creative expression to the world. Prophets have such acute giftings in this way. It is really important to understand this facet of your unique personality and role, as it is a part of your purpose and path on the earth.

Creation itself is in many ways a prophetic expression. God, being Spirit, called forth creation from nothing into something. But before He spoke out His Word to command the creation events, God saw things as though they were reality. Then God took clay in His hand and shaped the form of a perfect man, who He named Adam. Now before God breathed into the clay form and animated Adam, He had to see the man He was about to create.

If we look to the Scriptures, we see this clearly conveyed: "Before I formed you in the womb I knew you; before you were born I sanctified you; I ordained you a prophet to the nations" (Jeremiah 1:5). God is expressing that His insight goes to the point that He knows us personally before we are even created! As a prophet, you have the spiritual DNA of your Daddy. Like Father, like son. Like Father, like daughter. You carry His traits and creative expression in your nature.

Your prophetic gift operates in a mirror image to this nature of God. That's why many prophets are artistic, musical, creative, sculptors, actors, producers, directors or entrepreneurs. All of these roles complement the Father of heavenly lights, and are a reflection of His nature being expressed in and through us. It is not just that you have a wild imagination; it's that your prophetic gift adds to your talent levels and skills.

When the children of Israel chose to build a false idol after the Lord delivered them from Egyptian bondage, they did not choose the skilled artisans the Lord instructed Moses to use in building the first temple. Rather, they selected Aaron the high priest to craft an image of a calf out of gold. They used his creative anointing to build something they did not have. They didn't just appoint anyone; they appointed God's high priest. This is a picture and a warning of a perverted misuse of this prophetic creative gift (Exodus 31–32).

PROPHETIC CREATIVITY

God's Provision, Abundance, and Prosperity

In the story of Jacob, during his time working for Laban as a shepherd, we learn about his agreement with Laban to take ownership of any sheep and goats born with blemishes - which are referred to as the spotted and ring sheep and goats. Jacob used bark strips and set them up in front of the sheep at their watering trough where they daily gathered and drank. Those bark strips and branches were a prophetic act of faith, a representation of the stripes and blemishes he was believing for on the newborn animals.

As a result of this, an unusual percentage of the newborn livestock were born spotted and speckled, bizarrely transferring the strongest of the herd from a small percentage being blemished sheep to the majority being blemished. This caused Jacob to become rich and increase in livestock, according to his deal with his uncle Laban (Genesis 30:29–43).

God's Power and Authority

Moses went before Pharaoh and all of his sorcerers in the court (Exodus 7:1–12). Moses stood there on behalf of God, representing justice and freedom for the descendants of Abraham held captive. He was the predestined deliverer for Israel from the slavery of Egypt. As he stood there with Aaron, he had Aaron perform the simple task of throwing his staff on the floor. As he did so, the staff miraculously transformed into a snake. The sorcerers of Pharaoh's court replicated the demonstration of supernatural power; however, Moses's staff that had become a snake ate the other snakes that had come from the sorcerers' demonic power.

God's Protection

During the first Passover, God instructed the Israelite slaves to kill a lamb for each house, cook it in a specific way, and to take the blood and sprinkle it on the doorposts of the house (Exodus 12:1–14). This was a rather bizarre request by God, but it was the prophetic act of faith that the angel of the Lord would see when he visited Egypt that night to kill all the firstborn. He would spare only those who were inside houses with blood over the doors.

This seems odd, but those who painted their doors in the blood of the sacrificed animal were under God's protection. This was also a foretelling of the coming lamb of God in God's unique poetic style.

God's Healing

Moses was instructed by God to build a prophetic symbol by setting up a bronze serpent on a pole (Numbers 21:1–9). The people of Israel displeased God by complaining in transit to the Promise Land after being freed by Him from slavery in Egypt. God sent poisonous snakes, and the people were being bit and were dying.

God, in His mercy, responded by having Moses build the bronze snake and set it up on a pole. Once it was there, if people were bit, they only looked at the bronze snake and were healed!

This expression conveyed God's healing for His people, while at the same time prophetically and symbolically foretelling of Jesus who would also be hung on a tree for our salvation and redemption.

God's Instruction and Law

One example I love to think about is when Moses met God up Mount Sinai. God manifested His prophetic expression by cutting the rock face of the mountain and inscribing the Ten Commandments onto stone tablets. Moses walked away with tangible workmanship made by the hand of God Himself! This prophetic creativity made way for God's instruction and laws to be conveyed to us (Exodus 34:1).

An entire book would be required to list all the prophets who have impacted the world by obeying God's commands. There are so many facets around a prophet's various creative expressions.

WITTY IDEAS AND INVENTIONS

Inventions do not happen by themselves; rather, they are inspired ideas developed to change our lives, usually making our daily lives easier or more efficient. Noah was an inventor with a witty idea. He built something never before seen on the earth—a giant ocean-going vessel in the middle of a land-locked area. When I use the word *inventor*, I am referring to someone who is able to see something not in existence and then bring it into reality.

Noah was instructed by the Lord and given the dimensions and function of the ship we now know as the ark. My family built yachts when I was a young man, and I joined the business and went through all the formal training to become qualified as a shipbuilder. While I was training, I discovered the delicate science involved in the design and calculations of vessels, such as buoyancy and water displacement. The ark was the most perfect vessel ever built for its purpose. Its design specification is still relevant today.

Knowing what I know about designing and building boats, there is less than one in a million chance that a person who had never sailed before could guess something like a ship design that would not only float but withstand turbulent seas for an extended period of time. This is not to mention adding all the animals and people onboard. The tolerances in ship design are an exact science and not guesswork, or even educated guesswork, by any means. No, this was a God-given, Master-Craftsman, design.

Most people stop and admire the nice story about God saving Noah and his family through the flood. They do not press in to understand that God wants to download blueprints and details for them, just as He did for Noah. Each of us are given the same opportunity that Noah had to believe and act on God's word.

The truth is that we all need to follow in Noah's footsteps, hearing God's voice in such a way that something not yet seen can be birthed into the earth. If this world is just a dark shadow and a fraction of what heaven looks like, then there are endless inventions and witty ideas that can be accessed with hearing ears and seeing eyes.

Just a few years ago, there was a man in New Zealand who invented a stereo speaker system using water after he had dreams in which God instructed him on the design and production. That invention will ultimately bring great wealth to that man as he follows it through. Wealth in the hands of you, a child of God, will do great good and further the kingdom through evangelism, church buildings, orphanages, and an array of many other avenues. For you, this means the ability to be more available with your time to serve God in whatever way He leads.

In the early 1900s, my great-grandfather invented a device that brought boiling water straight into the kitchen. It led him to have one of the largest plumbing supply stores in New Zealand, due to the success he had at the time. Almost all hospitality restaurants or companies have one of these boiling devices, which has been a blessing to the world.

We know that God blessed Abraham "In blessing you I will bless all nations." The Jewish people are still reaping God's faithful promise to this day. Did you know that ninety percent of worldwide patents, which are like the copyrights to inventions, are held by Jewish people? Coincidence? I think not. Blessings come by God's design and covenant. The good news is that if you have given your life to Jesus, then you have been grafted into the vine of that covenant blessing God made with Abraham. You too are eligible to receive witty inventions and ideas from heaven.

It only takes hearing God clearly on one invention He is trying to show you for your entire world to change. Have you ever heard of or used peanut oil? If you have, then you can thank a gentleman by the name of George Washington Carver who lived in the early 1900s, in the same period that Henry Ford and Thomas Edison were creating history-changing inventions. Although Carver was known for peanut oil, he actually invented and discovered over three hundred various products mainly derived from peanuts, sweet potatoes, pecans, and soybeans. He always gave all the credit to God for showing him the ideas and was often noted saying, "God gave them to me." He asked the Lord to reveal to him creation's mysteries. God responded to say that He would reveal to Mr. Carver the mystery within the peanut. With that one revelation, he changed the world. Although he created three hundred products, he only ever patented three of them. His products not only were a blessing in his time, but they still bless the world today long after he passed.

In a similar way, I have asked God to speak clearly to me, tapping into what is available to me as a grafted son of Abraham's covenant. When I was twenty-four years old, I was in a partnership in a construction business that had 120 employees. My partner disappeared and stripped the company overnight, leaving me $750,000 in debt. I woke up to a nightmare of debt that I had no idea how I was going to pay off, since my company was completely sabotaged. I was in such turmoil, and my phone was ringing constantly with angry creditors, that I needed to get away from all the chaos.

With that situation, I saw my life through the lens of what had just happened coming to a complete halt without freedom or happiness ahead. I couldn't afford to even date, let alone marry. I never saw myself purchasing a house, having a nice car, vacationing, or anything else I had ever considered prior to losing everything in this business and going into debt.

While I was taking fifty calls a day from angry creditors, whom I had no answer for, I did something radical going against all logic—I took off five days. I flew up into the mountains of New Zealand with just my pack and rifle, to clearly hear God's voice. I was dropped off by a three-seater censor plane on a small bush landing runway in deserted mountains. I hiked for nine hours without seeing anyone, set up my tent, and spent the entire five days out of cellphone coverage, completely alone. Those days were spent crying out to God to rescue me and to speak to me about what I needed to do. I took my notepad with me, to collect my thoughts, but I ended up using it for what God started to speak to me.

I had two other small businesses at the time—a tiling installation business and a small residential construction business. At the time, they were barely surviving due to the huge loss resulting in a chain reaction across my financial landscape. I knew that within months, those two remaining companies would get buried in the burden of debt too. And then God started to speak to me.

God gave me an idea to diversify my tiling business into a business that serviced new and existing tiled surfaces and would eventually specialize in concrete flooring. God continued to speak to me. It was in my thoughts, but I knew it was the voice of God, so calm, collected, and ordered in what He was saying to me. I wrote everything down. He was not only showing me what to do but how to do it. God even went through all my costs in the new-concept service business. That encounter led to a new company model being birthed according to God's design.

In the two businesses I operated at that time, I was lucky to make 8–10 percent profit. The new business concept God was showing me made 50–75 percent profit.

I wrote everything down and, when I left the mountains, I flew out with hope and purpose. I had to work really hard to set everything up like God had shown me. I kept running my two other smaller companies and began to trade with this new service company. Not long after starting this new venture God had designed for me, I closed my other two businesses because this new God-breathed company was becoming so busy I wanted to give it my full attention.

Years later, when God moved me out to Orange County California to plant and pastor our church, I planted another branch of the company - proving it to be a successful business model outside of New Zealand. The company has, and continues to service, famous and well-known brands and locations. And I not only paid off the incredible debt I had, but it has been a great provision to my family. All this came from one encounter with God. Hearing God's witty idea not only changed my life but saved me financially from a crisis that was about to explode like a bomb on my life.

Just one moment of hearing God's voice can change everything.

How do you go about receiving a God idea? There are two different ways we can receive witty ideas or inventions from the

Lord. The first is in random selected moments where God decides to reveal His amazing wisdom into our lives. This can come about by thoughts, dreams, visions, or even interaction with the spiritual world. In these moments, we are usually not suspecting or expecting God to speak at all. But God in His goodness decides to meet us and generously entrust us with pearls that are seeds to revelation and breakthrough.

The second way God speaks is when we are aware of what we need for a breakthrough to occur, and we begin to seek God to solve a problem or challenge that is in front of us. For instance, there have been certain projects I have been involved with when a roadblock was met. Roadblocks not easily solved, and in fact they looked impossible to progress through. That is, they are impossible until the moment God provides the witty idea or invention that bridges the gaps between an island of impossible to the land of possible!

If you are believing for a business one day, one witty idea or invention blueprint from God can fast-track that. Did you ever stop to think what would happen if God gave you an invention that you copyrighted and patented? After that a contract giving the rights to production and distribution with royalties attached? Imagine if that one invention you received from God caused you to be paid just one dollar per item, but the company you signed rights to sold millions of units. That is inspiring.

Some people would say it's covetousness to focus on money, but I disagree. We are not focusing on the money here; we are focusing on money being a tool to further the gospel. It's not money that is evil, nor is it evil to have a lot of money. What is evil is the love of money and hoarding it for purposes that are not in line with God's will.

Hearing God in one moment can change your entire life and the lives of everyone around you ... if you are willing and obedient.

CHAPTER 10

THE CHURCH NEEDS PROPHETS

One thing that is certain is God always has something to say. There's also no doubt God has enabled all of us to hear His voice for ourselves, but that does not mean the church no longer needs prophets.

I always chuckle when I hear people suggesting the concept that the church no longer needs prophets today. We only need to read the history of God's children from Genesis, with Adam and Eve, through to the church of Laodicea in Revelation, to see that God's people often wander from His perfect design, plan, and will. It's in these seasons where we can read of a prophetic voice reminding God's people to return to His paths and instructions.

Today, in this generation, the church still needs prophets. Just as your body requires an array of minerals and nourishment to flourish in your day-to-day health, so God has seen that the bride, the body of Christ, also needs input specific to its needs, spiritual integrity, and health. God has ordained prophets to meet many of these needs.

Prophets have the role in the church of bringing fresh vision and promises corporately to the local and collective church body. God has anointed them to walk as watchmen who have eyes and ears tuned and sharpened to watch and listen, as guards for the enemy's assignments against, in, and around the church. Prophets are called to compel people not to leave the path of God's intent and commands, to stay true to the heavenly vision and mission.

Many pastors get concerned about prophets, because often some young or unwise prophet may behave in a way that negatively affects the church. But the Scriptures clearly give wisdom about this. Often, when church culture is not properly established it causes the mismanagement of prophets. Let's look at some biblical wisdom concerning this from 1 Corinthians 14:

> *"Pursue love, and desire spiritual gifts, but especially that you may prophesy. For he who speaks in a tongue does not speak to men but to God, for no one understands him; however, in the spirit he speaks mysteries. But he who prophesies speaks edification and exhortation and comfort to men. He who speaks in a tongue edifies himself, but he who prophesies edifies the church. I wish you all spoke with tongues, but even more that you prophesied; for he who prophesies is greater than he who speaks with tongues, unless indeed he interprets, that the church may receive edification.*
>
> *But now, brethren, if I come to you speaking with tongues, what shall it profit you unless I speak to you either by revelation, by knowledge, by prophesying, or by teaching? Even things without life, whether flute or harp, when they make a sound, unless they make a distinction in the sounds, how will it be known what is piped or played? For*

if the trumpet makes an uncertain sound, who will prepare for battle? So likewise you, unless you utter by the tongue words easy to understand, how will it be known what is spoken? For you will be speaking into the air. There are, it may be, so many kinds of languages in the world, and none of them is without significance. Therefore, if I do not know the meaning of the language, I shall be a foreigner to him who speaks, and he who speaks will be a foreigner to me. Even so you, since you are zealous for spiritual gifts, let it be for the edification of the church that you seek to excel.

Therefore let him who speaks in a tongue pray that he may interpret. For if I pray in a tongue, my spirit prays, but my understanding is unfruitful. What is the conclusion then? I will pray with the spirit, and I will also pray with the understanding. I will sing with the spirit, and I will also sing with the understanding. Otherwise, if you bless with the spirit, how will he who occupies the place of the uninformed say 'Amen' at your giving of thanks, since he does not understand what you say? For you indeed give thanks well, but the other is not edified.

I thank my God I speak with tongues more than you all; yet in the church I would rather speak five words with my understanding, that I may teach others also, than ten thousand words in a tongue.

Brethren, do not be children in understanding; however, in malice be babes, but in understanding be mature. In the law it is written: 'With men of other tongues and other lips I will speak to this people; and yet, for all that, they will not hear Me,' says the Lord.

Therefore tongues are for a sign, not to those who believe but to unbelievers; but prophesying is not for unbelievers but for those who believe. Therefore if the whole church comes together in one place, and all speak with tongues, and there come in those who are uninformed or unbelievers, will they not say that you are out of your mind? But if all prophesy, and an unbeliever or an uninformed person comes in, he is convinced by all, he is convicted by all. And thus the secrets of his heart are revealed; and so, falling down on his face, he will worship God and report that God is truly among you.

How is it then, brethren? Whenever you come together, each of you has a psalm, has a teaching, has a tongue, has a revelation, has an interpretation. Let all things be done for edification. If anyone speaks in a tongue, let there be two or at the most three, each in turn, and let one interpret. But if there is no interpreter, let him keep silent in church, and let him speak to himself and to God. Let two or three prophets speak, and let the others judge. But if anything is revealed to another who sits by, let the first keep silent. For you can all prophesy one by one, that all may learn and all may be encouraged. And the spirits of the prophets are subject to the prophets. For God is not the author of confusion but of peace, as in all the churches of the saints.

Let your women keep silent in the churches, for they are not permitted to speak; but they are to be submissive, as the law also says. And if they want to learn something, let them ask their own husbands at home; for it is shameful for women to speak in church.

Or did the word of God come originally from you? Or was it you only that it reached? If anyone thinks himself to be a prophet or spiritual, let him acknowledge that the things which I write to you are the commandments of the Lord. But if anyone is ignorant, let him be ignorant.

Therefore, brethren, desire earnestly to prophesy, and do not forbid to speak with tongues. Let all things be done decently and in order." (1 Corinthians 14:1-40).

The first comment I want to make and highlight is that the apostle Paul is making things clear here that God designed, ordained, and desires ... even demanding ... that prophecy happens in our churches. In fact, God *wants* to speak in His church. Limiting prophecy denies God His own voice in His own church. How could we ever think that we would have the right or the audacity to manipulate the voice and will of God out of our churches?

So, we can clearly conclude that when God wants to speak, it would be sinful to obstruct. Let's look a bit closer at a few key statements in the passage we just read:

- Let every prophecy be judged (or examined, assessed, and tested) by two or three others (verses 29–33).
- Let everything be done in decency and order (verse 40).
- The apparent goal of all gifts in the church is for the edification of the body; prophecy benefits the body.
- Chaos in the church because of the prophetic is not God's design. It must be carried out submitted to and with the goal of edifying the entire body. This does not mean flattery; sometimes, edification will actually be a confronting word.

KNOW THOSE WHO LABOR AMONG YOU

"And we urge you, brethren, to recognize those who labor among you, and are over you in the Lord and admonish you,

and to esteem them very highly in love for their work's sake. Be at peace among yourselves.

Now we exhort you, brethren, warn those who are unruly, comfort the fainthearted, uphold the weak, be patient with all. See that no one renders evil for evil to anyone, but always pursue what is good both for yourselves and for all.

Rejoice always, pray without ceasing, in everything give thanks; for this is the will of God in Christ Jesus for you.

Do not quench the Spirit. Do not despise prophecies. Test all things; hold fast what is good. Abstain from every form of evil" (1 Thessalonians 5:12–22).

Paul commands us "to know those that labor among you." Now, we normally reflect on this scripture when referring to leadership and ministers, but I want to discuss this passage through the perspective of prophecy.

Too often in our generation, people and churches are far too eager to let anyone minister in the prophetic. This is one of the contributing factors to mistrust and damage in the church. Or worse, prophets are not honored as a necessity for direction and edification, but are a sideshow for church entertainment and wow factors. We need to know those that labor among us. Often, I have seen complete strangers standing up in church services trying to release prophetic words, but they have no planting or submission to that community. This is dangerous.

I have also seen this on a level that self-proclaimed prophets have staged personal prophecy over individuals they really have no connection to and no real authority to release words over. I have had well-known ministers come into our church and release words over people that should have never been released. A prophetic person can possibly perceive a destiny word over congregational members; however, some people are not in a right place yet to hear these words. So even though there may be truth to these prophecies, it can end up doing more damage than good.

As an example, I have had visiting ministers come in and try to commission some of my young disciples to get up and go to the nations, when they clearly were not ready for that. Their character was still in need of oversight and maturity. It's easy to walk into a church congregation that isn't yours and release "powerful words" that sound impressive and with anointing to match, over people; however, when there is no accountability to grow that person into the word of God released. The visiting prophesying minister gets to move on to the next city, the next day, with no responsibility.

The church needs prophets, but it does not need unwise ministers and prophets claiming to have the word of the Lord with zero responsibility for the future well-being of the congregation. We do not need prophets rolling in to unleash false expectations and words out of season to people.

Truth acknowledges destiny but grounds that word in maturity, submission, and training. People love to issue the big "sending" and "go now" prophecies, but we must know those who labor among us in regards to prophetic words. If we fail to do this, we may get caught up dealing with someone who wants to walk in the power of prophecy but not the responsibility for the soul and future of that life.

I have had this cause damage numerous times over the years in our church, so now I simply ask visiting ministers to run those destiny words past myself or my wife before they seed people with those words. We must know the credibility and wisdom of those who labor among us and in our church communities, so we can avoid damage and mistrust toward the genuine prophetic gifts in our midst.

DON'T QUENCH THE SPIRIT AND DON'T DESPISE PROPHECY

Paul urges us not to quench the Holy Spirit. This means that we do not grieve or hurt Him by conflicting with His will. Paul is advising us not to "squash" His plans by pushing our own plans forward.

Then Paul tells us "not to despise prophesying." Just because we had a bad experience with prophecy does not mean we should take offence or prejudice toward it. It is God's design to channel His voice and plans over our lives and communities through a mouthpiece, His specific "Jeremiah 29:11" over each of us.

We can never claim that it is maturity or wisdom to despise something because of a bad experience. Your bad experience was a lesson, but you will only benefit properly from it if you choose to let God heal your heart, and make the decision to trust again. This is why Paul tells us to "test all things, [and] hold fast to what is good." We are not to be naïve and gullible. We are to be good stewards of our lives. We must test prophecies that come in our churches. We are instructed to test everything that comes and, as the old saying goes, "eat the meat and spit out the bones." Do not just consume everything given to you; test what's given to make sure that it is actually a Spirit-breathed word and not just hot air.

WE DESPERATELY NEED PROPHETS

The church desperately needs prophets as much as it needs pastors, evangelists, apostles, and teachers. As the church, we must learn to value the prophets in our midst at the different levels of maturity and platforms they have. We must allow prophets opportunity to use their gifts. If we do not, then how will maturity come? After all, the pastor and preacher were not seasoned in their first sermon and probably made a whole list of blunders, that years later they are embarrassed about. I have my own list when I think back to my first time preaching.

We must create environments of opportunity where young prophets can step out and take risks, while learning to prophesy to us and our people. That does not mean we give them a platform before they are ready, qualified, or seasoned. But we can create an opportunity where they are safe to get it wrong and learn from their mistakes. They will gradually become more accurate as they exercise and practice their prophetic skills under the guidance of seasoned, veteran prophets.

Like any organization, the church must always pay attention to training the next generation of disciples. Merely celebrating the heroes of the previous or current season, will never make way for the heroes and pillars of the church in tomorrow's season. Only opportunity, environment, care, guidance, counsel, and wisdom will make that possible.

The body of Christ needs the prophetic voice that will announce what is being seen and ensure that vision is fulfilled and crises are averted. As a church body, we must regain our respect and value of the prophets in our midst, giving them their voices back, where previously control and fear removed them.

Learn wisdom in facilitating opportunity for prophets who are within your community to speak and grow in their gift and calling. You may want to have a prophetic team meet periodically and teach prophets from material like this book series. But make sure it is more than just head knowledge. It must be practically learned too. It may look like all of your young prophets and prophetic people sitting in a room and practicing obtaining prophetic words for each other. Find where they are able to function healthily and then start from that level in training.

Before someone stands up in your Sunday morning service with a word for your entire church, he or she must be proven faithful, on lower level prophetic responsibility to individuals, before being trusted with an entire congregation. Allow time and seasoning to take root in people so that you can learn to trust them. Accuracy in more than one instance is imperative. I have seen backslidden Christians, practicing all kinds of sin, produce accurate words. It is okay to require trust of a prophet's sincerity, humility, care for the hearers, fear of the Lord, and intimate personal lives with

Him. Learn to look for these qualities in their lives when they do not think anyone is watching. If you find the quality is there, you will be blessed at what comes out of their mouths when everyone is watching and listening.

Be gracious when prophets make mistakes. Remember they are people too. Do not chase prophets out of your churches, for in doing so, you may also lose the reward that leaves with them. You may lose blessing of the sight they carry or can carry if you give them the space and time to grow.

Prophecies can fail. So, if someone delivers a prophetic word that does not come to pass, take it to the Lord in prayer and ask Him. Do not be critical. In the same manner, if a prophet delivers a word not accompanied by the Holy Spirit or in contradiction with the Word of God, that prophet must be humble enough to admit the error and set things right with the hearers. It's simple really: prophets are not gods; they are messengers *for* God.

Make room for the prophetic gifts to speak into your community. As a result, you will experience a new level of breakthrough and heavenly insight, as we each do our best to follow the path of God together.

CHAPTER 11

WHAT EVERY CHURCH LEADER WANTS YOU TO KNOW

Many church leaders have had bad experiences with people claiming to be prophets. Or perhaps, some church leaders have experienced juvenile prophets who claim to carry authority but instead make big messes. This is unfortunate.

Bad experiences do not take away the reality that church leaders need prophets in their churches. It is true that prophets operate at different appropriate capacities and levels of maturity as they grow. What church leaders do not need, however, are prophets causing chaos in their church communities. As both a prophet and the senior pastor of a church, I think I can offer some keen insights into this area.

Leaders need prophets, but they do not need prophetic individuals operating out of a Jezebel-spirited nature. Leaders do not need so-called prophets controlling through spiritual manipulation. As a prophet, your gift is there to serve the leadership of the church and the people to whom you minister; you are not to control. You have been given gifts to build up and strengthen people and churches, not to override and undermine appointed authority. So, let us get into breaking down what every church leader wants you to know.

ESSENTIAL WISDOM IS REQUIRED FOR A DEVELOPING PROPHET

The fact is you are going to make mistakes. It's going to happen in your journey of walking with God, growing as a son or daughter of the King, and developing the gifts and callings in your life. And this is going to happen, *especially* as it relates to developing in your call as a prophet.

The key to not destroying your future is to walk out these mistakes with a teachable, humble spirit and a soft heart. Many times, when we are growing, we make the mistake of being bold without humility. We feel the need to defend our prophetic word or opinion to the death because we said "God is saying" preceding what we announced. If pride is present and we get things wrong, we often will not want to admit it because of embarrassment and shame. All this is done is the name of being a strong and bold prophet. When a prophet refuses to humble him or herself, people get hurt and become casualties. And the fact is local pastors are left to clean up the mess of "Thus saith the Lord."

You may have heard the quote, "Fake it until you make it." It's the concept of making it look good, even if you don't know what you're doing; pretend or guess until you start getting it right. But we simply cannot allow this culture or concept to be present in our lives, nor does it have any place in the prophetic gifts or office. In fact, this practice should not be functioning anywhere in the kingdom of God. When we get it wrong, we must be humble enough to admit and acknowledge it, thus defusing the statement that has just been spoken with an appearance of authority. And, in some cases, apologies must be made. We cannot ever allow our ego and pride to be more valuable than the outcome of another's life. We must not be so full of ourselves as to mishandle the words of God as if they are our own.

When we walk in foolishness, ignorance, and reckless conduct while displaying the "badge" of a prophet, over time making continual messes, we start to gain a bad reputation. Mistrust, and even levels of prejudice, can be established by others around us, even extending to leaders and pastoral nurturers.

Always remember that, as a prophet, you are the messenger and not the source of the voice or the power of God itself. Continually look for confirmation to verify the accuracy of what you believe you are discerning from the Lord. Learn the art of delivering God's message with boldness while postured in a place of humility.

UNDERSTANDING, DISCRETION, AND WISDOM

Knowing or seeing something is not always the release to speak it, or to even let on that you know or sense what is taking place. It is just as important to know when to speak and share as to know what it is that you have seen or heard from God. Proverbs reminds us that discretion will keep us (Proverbs 2:11). It will keep us from harm and all kinds of awkward and uncomfortable situations, accusations, and broken relationships.

Timing is the element used in surprise. One of God's "suddenly" moments, and a prophet with no discretion can do more damage than good. This poor timing is often the mistake of a young prophet in training or of an immature prophet who lacks the maturity obtained from feeding on the Word of God and spiritual things.

In World War II, the common Allied slogan in the intelligence department was "Loose lips sink ships." One word spoken out of pride or foolishness can cause huge wounds, rejection, offences, and division. For instance, you might perceive something in someone indicating they have a particular sin or stronghold issue. That person might not be ready to hear what you see, or perhaps you do not have the right to speak into their life. Speaking into someone's life without the Holy Ghost's and local authorities' green light could cause a slew of repercussions. The recipient could rise up with major offence, a huge wound inflicted, and the access to speak into that person's life will be closed for a long time. That person could completely reject what you say and not receive anything from others or God in that area at all. They may actually get into a worse state because a prophet did not operate in full discernment!

Nathan the prophet did not show up and confront David when he was on the rooftop looking over to Bathsheba. Nor did Nathan come when David sent her husband to the front line so he would die. He came *after* David had moved her into the palace and was living out the repercussions of his sin. This was God's timing. It was here where David was in a place to listen; prior to then, in the heat of the moment or in the middle of the act, David may have not heard. His heart might not have received God's rebuke.

I think it would be fair to say that we have all met people who do not know how to stop talking and everything they know comes out of their mouth with no filter.

Understanding when to talk, who to talk to, and how much to say is a matter of maturity. While a fool can hold their tongue and *seem* wise, *understanding* a matter and truly being wise comes from being established in the Spirit of wisdom through relationship with the person of the Holy Spirit. It takes wisdom to operate in discretion. When we get this, our words will be selected carefully and placed at the right time, in the appropriate situation, when the hearer will actually value or benefit from what is being said.

If words in excess or foolishness have been spoken discrediting your reputation, character, honor, or integrity, then people may not receive what you have to say, even if it may be wise. If you have the opportunity to humble yourself before these people, take it. It's much better to eat humble pie than it is to silence God's voice or become hard and operate out of a gift without God's blessing.

James talks about how sweet and bitter waters cannot flow from the same spring (James 3:11). Make sure you have consistency and do not put on your prophetic spiritual hat only when you want to be heard, while acting foolishly and discrediting yourself at other times. True wisdom and maturity cause consistency in your walk, both spiritually and non-spiritually. This demonstrates a grounded stability that people will honor and listen to.

For example, imagine an aspiring young man who has the most brilliant business plan and wants to present it to a Fortune 500 company. It won't matter how amazing his business presentation is if he arrives to the boardroom in rags and smells, after not showering for weeks. No one will listen to him. Why? Because he will be perceived as someone who has no credibility. Thoughts will go through the Fortune 500 companies board members minds like, "This guy stinks. If he cannot present his own self respectably, then why should we listen to his thoughts on business?" In the same way, the way we present ourselves makes a difference. Wisdom and discretion will keep and guard us and cause us to prosper not only in our prophetic gifting and ministry, but also in our life!

In Proverbs 25:11, we read "a word fitly spoken in due season is like apples of gold in settings of silver." Ask the Holy Spirit to teach you and guide you into maturity and cause you to think and operate with both wisdom and discretion.

THE TIMING AND JUDGEMENT OF A MATTER

One of the hallmarks of someone who has matured in this office is he or she will discern both the timing and judgement of a matter.

It seems easier to understand God's plan in many cases than it is to understand God's timing for that particular plan.

On one hand, we must discern and know whether what God has shown us is meant to be spoken now, later, or held back. And on the other hand, we must discern the timeframe of that word being properly received. There were many times when I was young when I blurted out the right thing at the wrong time. I have already expressed that the right piece of information at the wrong time can cause chaos and inflict pain in people's hearts.

Some words are not meant to be spoken in the moment, present season, or while a person's heart is not be ready or able to receive. As mature prophets, the word is to be kept with discretion. We, as prophets, must be able to discern and inquire when, or if at all, that word should be spoken.

We have all either been, or can think of, people who are not ready to hear certain things. God's words released in the wrong time can cause people to run away or rebel against the word, and in some cases, it even causes the hearer to become conceited. Correct timing and judgement of a matter requires of us the art of being sensitive enough to walk tenderly with the Holy Spirit in such a way that when we sense Him leading us to share, then we share. But if we feel Him putting a check in our heart, then we hold back until we feel Him release us to speak it out.

Even though we as prophets are privileged to see past some of the layers of situations and lives, we do not see every single detail.

This is why it is so important that we rely on the Holy Spirit to lead and guide us as to how we minister.

We also need to understand the best possible timeframe for the revelation we are receiving. Most of the time, when God speaks, we interpret the revelation to mean an immediate result or delivery. And in the majority of these situations, we find ourselves or others left confused or disappointed. Delivering a prophetic word in such a way that deposits faith, without overpromising timeframes, is another important aspect of wisdom.

Young and developing prophets can often display this immature attribute of blurting out whatever it is they discern the moment they discern it. It is great that you are hearing from God, just do not inflict damage, pain, or chaos on others by speaking out everything you hear.

When I was young in the prophetic calling in my own life, I would feel compelled to speak out approximately ninety-five percent of everything I heard or saw in the Spirit. Now, years later, I usually only speak out approximately five to ten percent of what I hear ... even though I hear and discern so much more than I did years earlier. I have learned it's not all for the world around me. Sometimes, God reveals things so I can know how to interact, respond, and pray into life unfolding around me.

The first example we can see of this is in the life of a well-trained disciple, Elisha. His mentor, Elijah, was about to be taken up to heaven. When Elisha came to Bethel, the school of the prophets had accurate words of knowledge that his master would be received up to heaven, and yet in both cases Elisha told them to be quiet.

> *"Then Elijah said to Elisha, 'Stay here, please, for the* LORD *has sent me on to Bethel.'*
>
> *But Elisha said, 'As the* LORD *lives, and as your soul lives, I will not leave you!' So they went down to Bethel.*
>
> *Now the sons of the prophets who were at Bethel came out to Elisha, and said to him, 'Do you know that the* LORD *will take away your master from over you today?'*
>
> *And he said, 'Yes, I know; keep silent!'*
>
> *Then Elijah said to him, 'Elisha, stay here, please, for the* LORD *has sent me on to Jericho.'*
>
> *But he said, 'As the* LORD *lives, and as your soul lives, I will not leave you!' So they came to Jericho.*
>
> *Now the sons of the prophets who were at Jericho came to Elisha and said to him, 'Do you know that the* LORD *will take away your master from over you today?'*
>
> *So he answered, "Yes, I know; keep silent!" (2 Kings 2:2-5).*

Knowing something in the spirit is not always free license to speak it out.

Jesus knew who His betrayer was well in advance of Judas actually betraying Him—even before the Last Supper where He cryptically described who it was who would betray Him. When He was sitting at the Last Supper with Judas still at the table, John tells us what happened:

"I do not speak concerning all of you. I know whom I have chosen; but that the Scripture may be fulfilled, He who eats bread with Me has lifted up his heel against Me. Now I tell you before it comes, that when it does come to pass, you may believe that I am He. Most assuredly, I say to you, he who receives whomever I send receives Me; and he who receives Me receives Him who sent Me.'

When Jesus had said these things, He was troubled in spirit, and testified and said, 'Most assuredly, I say to you, one of you will betray Me.' Then the disciples looked at one another, perplexed about whom He spoke." (John 13:18-22).

Even when Jesus was facing extreme circumstances, He used great wisdom and discretion when releasing prophetic revelation. We all must learn from this example.

PROPHETIC ETIQUETTE

Submitting to established and appointed leadership is of the utmost importance for the prophet. There is a right way and a wrong way to approach access in order to minister in any capacity to another leader's congregation. Where us prophets can go wrong is to assume that our message is so important that it warrants bypassing protocol and honor toward those who stand in the positions of responsibility over the trusting lives of their flock.

Generally, most prophets are not pastoral in nature. Consequently, some prophets will overlook the need for nurture and long-term care for the lives of the people they interact with prophetically. Pastors will often be the ones to come to the aid of those in their churches who have received reckless and unwise prophecies and prophetic advice. The source of this is usually young, immature, or zealous prophets who do not understand the prophetic principles of etiquette.

Mistrust and disdain toward prophets, from many in the office of a pastor, stem from this lack of etiquette. Prophetic etiquette is the respect and honor of protocol and conduct that will cause a smooth delivery of your ministry, all without allowing room for foolishness, arrogance, or disregard.

Our goal as prophets is to insightfully walk within the lanes that we are given by the pastor or congregation we are ministering to. We should submit to whatever the local pastor is comfortable with us doing. The crux of this is prophetic etiquette is about learning the language of humility and honor. Honor your hearers with the same passion that burns inside of you to deliver the message.

Etiquette is the understanding that not everything you discern must be said the moment you discern it. This was a mistake I made many times early in my walk as a prophet. If your pastor releases you but puts requirements on how, where, and when you may minister, then respect and submit to his or her request.

You may have a gift, and even an accurate one, but your pastor assesses your character and integrity aside from your gift. He or she will be watching how well you honor the requirements put on you, and how well you also care for those you are ministering to. Remember a prophet does not have the right to just show up to a meeting and start issuing words to anyone he or she sees fit. As a pastor, I would immediately put a stop to this kind of behavior. Without any knowledge of the person prophesying, I could be exposing my people to great error. And that is not acceptable in our house.

Immature prophets can tend to behave in this insensitive manner, conflicting with congregational guidance and advice, and creating a gulf between what a prophet said and what a pastor's heart advises in nurturing care. Prophets can simply show up and deliver a word and move on to the next person, but a pastor, on the other hand, must walk a person through the process and journey they are on. True pastors become familiar with the unique needs, weaknesses, strengths, and insights of people's lives. They form deep and intimate concern for their flock's well-being. They take their roles as shepherds seriously.

Pastors have firsthand understanding of the fallout people experience when a prophet comes to town with a "thus saith the Lord" word over them. Perhaps the word pricks people's pride, causing rebellion, hurts their feelings in delivery, or causes them to run off into the distance with a word that perhaps God did not intend to fulfill for another twenty years. Pastors understand the process and the time it takes to see prophetic words manifest into the natural. So, while you have blown in and blown minds, pastors need your honor because they know their sheep and want them all to make it in the long run. If you have been given access and permission to speak, then take it seriously. It is a huge honor.

Prophets have an unfortunate character reputation for being lone rangers. Trouble with protocol, integrity, and submission are the calling cards of immature prophets. Good pastors will put requirements on young developing prophets with the best interest of those in attendance to meetings and congregation members. It also acts as a safety net for a prophet as well. It creates a safe space for the words to be tested and the prophet to have feedback and learn.

Make it your mission to be a prophet known for your honor. Do all you can to find out what the prophetic culture is in your church community. If you do not know, then ask your pastor or resident prophets in the church and begin to grasp it. Ask the Holy Spirit to guide you in each case where you have given a prophetic word. The goal is not to cause trouble because of dishonor but rather to strengthen, equip, and cooperate by blessing church leaders.

CHAPTER 12

WHAT IS PROPHETIC MATURITY?

For most of us, when we look at prophetic maturity, the most common definition that comes to mind is the skill level or accuracy of the prophet. Contrary to most of our initial conclusions, we will discover that accuracy and maturity are not one in the same. Prophetic maturity is somewhat connected to accuracy and becoming skilled in hearing or seeing various forms of messages from the Lord, but maturity has more to do with submission and obedience to carrying out what God requires of us.

Maturity is closely linked to learning stewardship of what we hear and see, walking in wisdom distributing heaven's insight or instruction, and standing with humility in our roles and authority. We learn how to temper our gift, role, and identity in learning to walk in love and wisdom. What do I mean by learning to love?

LOVE MATURELY

By nature, many prophets can be explosive and fiery. It's part of our makeup. And this is not a character defect; God wishes us to use that to be bold and speak for Him. It's a typical characteristic that you will find in someone with this calling. Love, on the other hand, is a mark of maturity in a prophet.

It is easy for prophets to see through supernatural insight into what may seem to them as simple answers from God's perspective. It appears to them, that people are constantly going in the opposite direction and making bad decisions, thus rejecting and despising them for bringing the word of the Lord. While prophets usually see black and white, right and wrong, pointing out absolutes, the mark of maturity is how well they respond to their treatment. Prophets are rejected for many reasons, but a true prophet is able to guard his or her heart, stay soft, and tuned to God's voice for others.

As a prophet, you do not want to become hard in your heart. Again, it does not matter how mature and skilled you are in an area of the prophetic; if you do not learn how to walk in love, then you will never be a mature prophet. Without love, you will live on low-level gifts and never be trusted with true promotion by God. If you cannot be trusted to submit to pastoral leaders, guard your heart from wounds and offences, and keep your heart soft toward others so that your anointing is not tainted, then you will not progress in your calling. In fact, you are in danger of operating out of a gift rather than the unction of the Holy Spirit.

When I was younger in the prophetic, growing as a son of God but also as a young prophet, my perspective was quite different than what it is now. Back then, I thought that the weightier matters were the level of anointing I would need to carry as I grew and the price of things I would need to sacrifice were going to be the most difficult to walk into and attain. But I was wrong. I found out learning to love people is an internal crucifixion process and the most difficult. When mistreated, especially as a prophet, we want to retaliate and respond, defend ourselves, and fight for our honor to be restored. How wrong this is.

God's idea of maturity is actually being able to turn the other cheek, to respond in forgiveness, and to not hold grudges when treated badly. To be like this, we must not satisfy our emotional demands, as we read:

> *"My son, pay attention to what I say; turn your ear to my words. Do not let them out of your sight, keep them within your heart; for they are life to those who find them and health to one's whole body. Above all else, guard your heart, for everything you do flows from it. Keep your mouth free of perversity; keep corrupt talk far from your lips"* (Proverbs 4:20–24).

Clearly outlined in verse 23, great emphasis is placed on guarding your heart. It does not say avoid being around, interacting with, or ministering to those who may reject or hurt you. Rather, we are to guard our hearts. Our job, the job of any prophet or child of God for that matter, is to obey the word and instruction of God. This obedience includes all Scripture, regardless of how people treat us.

As Proverbs 4:23 instructs us, we must guard our hearts so that in the process of hurting situations, words, and hostilities, we can remain vulnerable enough to protect, care for, and love, but guarded enough to not allow emotions and feelings from others to impact our heart, value, or identity. Before you can grow in maturity, you will need to grow in love. It takes more strength to operate in love than in rage. That is why a true mark of a prophet is how well he or she loves, because it demonstrates that the prophet has been through the process of God's refining, and thus I can feel confident in their care for others.

This is not the type of love that comes easy. This is the kind of mature love we must pursue and seek that actually causes us to lay our lives down for our friends, much like Jesus did. Even when we do not feel like those hurting us are our friends, we must remember that as Jesus hung dying on a cross, held there by love, all of His friends had abandoned Him in His darkest moment. All except John. Jesus was ultimately betrayed into the position of the cross by one of His close friends and disciples - Judas. And yet there was not an ounce of bitterness in Jesus. He went to the cross, He died on the cross, forgiving.

This is how we to grow in love maturity. We learn to stay silent in the face of our accusers, to not respond to hostility or try to defend ourselves. The reality is we can grow in skill with opportunity and time, but maturity is not gained in the same way. Have you ever seen bodybuilders? It is not in a state of rest, pleasure, or peace that growth takes place. Muscle growth only occurs when resistance is in effect. It is only when people lift weights that muscles are stretched and grown. We do not usually grow in our life when all is well. Adversity, as it turns out, is the breeding ground for growth.

It's important to note that growth does not just occur from walking through trials; growth and maturity are increased by walking through trials with a right posture, attitude, and heart. It takes walking in real love to not respond out of wounds or pain, lashing out in the trial we are walking through. James 1:2–4 has encouraged me countless times regards to this:

> *"My brethren, count it all joy when you fall into various trials,*
> *knowing that the testing of your faith produces patience. But*
> *let patience have its perfect work, that you may be perfect*
> *and complete, lacking nothing" (James 1:2–4).*

As we progress, growing into the maturity of loving well, our perspective and motives begin to change. We grow from the young zealous prophet who is absorbed with our own prophetic anointing and how important our prophetic words are - a place where we tend to see people as problems and abrasive - to a fulfilled prophetic ministry where we view people as God's sheep and we are the directors on the road to where they are headed. This is one of the primary reasons why prophets take years to mature, not weeks or months through a course, internship, or a class. Growing in love is a process of unlearning immature, abrasive, and youthful characteristics.

As we begin to grow in this area of authentic love, we recognize those around us, who we serve and minister to, through the heart of the Father. We begin to see people with compassion, patience, and understanding, and with the optimistic love of God. It's not that we lose our boldness, it's that we must lose our harshness.

Understand that each person, people group, or community we minister and interact with, Jesus Himself personally bled and died for, and has the value of the life that Jesus laid down. We must not become intoxicated with the apparent greatness of our gifting or prophetic insight and lose sight of the value of each life we serve and minster to. We all have lost sight at times, but we must recognize the prophetic ministry as a sober and weighty responsibility. Cain was wrong, we are our brother's keeper (Genesis 4).

Love does not ignore issues; it is gracious and rejoices in the truth. As prophets, God wants us to represent His heart and not His judgement. This does not mean we should not deliver correction when He leads us, but it does mean we are not to be harsh or unloving in the handling of people's hearts. God is always dealing with us in the language of redemption. Love is like that. Love will be tough at times and even extremely confrontational, but always with the objective of getting the individual to their destination of promise.

Wise people embrace loving and stern correction, knowing that godly correction is never intended to harm, punish, or control, but rather to bring freedom, healing, and destiny a little closer. But remember not everyone God is sending you to, to deliver the word of the Lord, is wise. Some of them have little wisdom. So, guard your heart.

Your prophetic gift must always be channeled through God's heart and ultimate love for people, no matter what type of word is being delivered.

THE WAY OF WISDOM

Growing in the prophetic means growing in wisdom. After all, one of the three prophetic gifts of the Spirit is wisdom (Isaiah 11:1–2). The word of wisdom is divine wisdom unctioned in a prophetic word for the moment. It's an amazing channel that God will speak through from time to time, but it is not a mentality of learned wisdom that alters our perspective. It must be acquired.

Prophetic maturity is just as much grounded in wisdom as it is in love. We're not speaking here of the gift of the word of wisdom, but about the wisdom that comes when you spend lots of time with God. It changes the way you see and perceive.

Lack of wisdom will always be obvious. Shame and pain are not far away from this situation. When we start out, we think that as soon as we hear or see something prophetically, we are to blurt it out and it will cause instant change or amaze people that God is speaking through us. The need for the adrenalin rush of prophetic power and attention in an unseasoned prophet will override the wisdom needed to responsibly steward the gift, and ultimately affect the hearts and lives of the people around.

Wisdom teaches us not just *what* to speak from the perspective of accuracy but also *when* to speak. Timing is everything to God.

Hastiness is a near guarantee that trouble is close. Wisdom will instruct us to become masters of *who* needs to hear the matter, but discretion will keep you and guard you in all your ways. No one who had a loose tongue was ever trusted with weighty matters, as they were perceived as a fool. However, when we make prophetic ministry mistakes, mature wisdom will help us to make the situation right, protecting our hearts through the process of humbly correcting as needed. We are capable of walking in wisdom, coupled with humility to take responsibility for our errors or moments of failure.

If you have a tantrum in front of people, even in a subtle way, and you expose your true immaturity, can you expect that people will respect and receive from your so-called spiritual prophetic authority? The weighty words you deliver will be measured by your behavior. And your behavior is always being measured, not just in the prophetic moment.

Likewise, I've previously explained that knowing when *not* to speak is also wisdom. Those who are really close to me have recognized that I do not share most of what I prophetically hear, perceive, or see. This is because if I revealed everything I discerned or received prophetically, it could cause damage, rejection, or even sabotage to the process God is trying to work in people's lives. Premature truth in the wrong situation can be much more damaging than almost anything else. Young prophets take a while to learn this because their zeal and pride will often override this truth, due to their need to be recognized as someone who can accurately hear God. As we mature in this wisdom, we will begin to become excellent stewards of understanding what is being revealed to us to be passed on to specific people, and what is for our own understanding.

I remember when the Holy Spirit gave me a revelation about this truth. I was reflecting on an unhealthy prophetic culture I had been observing for a while and was becoming bothered by it. The Holy Spirit perfectly described to me what I was seeing and thinking about. I call it my "sons of the prophet's revelation." Let's take a look as I explain this revelation using the last chapter of Elijah's life as found in 2 Kings:

> *"And it came to pass, when the LORD was about to take up Elijah into heaven by a whirlwind, that Elijah went with Elisha from Gilgal. Then Elijah said to Elisha, 'Stay here, please, for the LORD has sent me on to Bethel.'*
>
> *But Elisha said, 'As the LORD lives, and as your soul lives, I will not leave you!' So they went down to Bethel.*
>
> *Now the sons of the prophets who were at Bethel came out to Elisha, and said to him, 'Do you know that the LORD will take away your master from over you today?'*
>
> *And he said, 'Yes, I know; keep silent!'*
>
> *Then Elijah said to him, 'Elisha, stay here, please, for the LORD has sent me on to Jericho.'*
>
> *But he said, 'As the LORD lives, and as your soul lives, I will not leave you!' So they came to Jericho.*

Now the sons of the prophets who were at Jericho came to Elisha and said to him, 'Do you know that the LORD will take away your master from over you today?'

So he answered, 'Yes, I know; keep silent!'" (2 Kings 2:1–5).

Do you notice that in both Bethel and Jericho there was a school of the prophets? It was a gathering of young zealous prophets, learning the prophetic. In both cases, prophets from the schools of Bethel and Jericho prophesied eagerly and accurately. But in both cases, Elisha told them, "I know, stay silent." In other words, they were speaking something he already knew.

Not everything that we can prophesy should be spoken! But what the Holy Spirit told me was so much deeper than that. He said to me, "Andrew, accurate prophecy is entry-level prophetic involvement." Elisha was in pursuit of so much more than just an accurate word of knowledge; he was in pursuit of a much more mature reward. He was chasing encounter and impartation.

In our prophetic culture today, I see the word of knowledge being displayed like the pinnacle of prophetic spirituality; however, we have much to learn in pursuit of the advanced matters of the prophetic. Understanding the wisdom of God in this area will equip us to become skillful deliverers of prophetic messages. Knowing *how* to speak to an individual, even down to the details such as our tone and body language, will cause us to be received and listened to.

A doctor will spend approximately seven years training just to get out of school and into the workplace. Doctors must learn their skill of practice perfectly. And on par with learning skills, doctors must also learn how to work with compassion and care toward their patients. In fact, in the United States, doctors take an oath to serve and care for their patients. It's required of them that they handle each patient and patient's family as best suits from case to case. You may have heard the term "bedside manner."

In the same way, it's not just your skill set as a prophet that matters. It's your prophetic bedside manner. No one likes to receive from, or be in the company of, an accurate prophet who is harsh and unloving. Prophetic maturity is not just about doing your job; it's about doing it with love and care for those you minister to.

You may be wondering at this point, "How and when will I attain all of these necessary things?" And I have a very simple answer for you, which is found in the book of James: "If any of you lacks wisdom, let him ask of God, who gives to all liberally and without reproach, and it will be given to him" (James 1:5). God will freely give you wisdom if you ask Him. It may take some time and even a process to gain that wisdom, but it will be gained if you ask.

The book of Proverbs instructs us: "In all your getting, get understanding" (Proverbs 4:7). The Holy Spirit is your guide and will be with you every step of the way. He wants you to obtain these areas of growth more than you want them. As you submit to Him, the peace that passes understanding will guard your heart and your mind in Christ Jesus, making sense of prophetic growth as you embrace it. Prophetic maturity embraces authentic love and gains God-given wisdom.

CHAPTER 13

START AT THE LEVEL YOU ARE NOW AT

All of us want to get to the level of maturity we feel is required for the fullness of our call as fast as possible. But the reality is that things of value always take time. Time, discipline, and focus are ingredients for greatness and development—they cannot be bypassed if we want to obtain the genuine article.

David was anointed to be king by Samuel the prophet when he was a young boy. I am sure from that moment onward, he internally felt like a king on the inside, but his external reality did not yet reflect that, and it would not for several years. You may be in a similar process directly related to your calling as a prophet. You may feel like you're already at the destination of what God has promised you. Or perhaps you have an agitation to get to where you are going. But you cannot skip steps in God's preparation journey ... if you want to truly do things God's way.

Maybe you are just starting to realize God's calling as a prophet over your life. You may be having glimpses into the future of your calling and destiny. God wants that vision to hold fast in your heart. And, at the same time, He wants you to embrace all of what He has in the present season today.

The fact is that God wants you to learn and grow. And to do that, you are going to need to start learning at the gifting and authority level you are at today. God wants to see if you will be just as content and faithful serving in your local church, in less glamorous areas, as you would be being used by Him in the greatness of notable moments in the prophetic. Be faithful with the little—stay faithful—and you will become ruler over much more and begin to realize the greater aspects of your gifting, calling, and office in which you stand.

Take risks as you learn to step out in prophetic words of knowledge and seeing into the spirit realm. It's okay to get it wrong! Just be humble if you get it wrong, and learn from what you can improve on next time. Stay humble and God will lead you and teach you ... and use you. Develop your relationship with the Holy Spirit. He is your ultimate teacher.

The Holy Spirit is going to introduce you into all the aspects of the prophetic realm and lead you into gifts and dimensions of God's kingdom you did not even know existed. You will learn so much from the mentor that God will give you. If you do not have a mentor yet, pray and ask God for one. Ask God for someone who is mature and will teach you and care for your development.

It has often been said that the journey of a thousand miles begins with the first step. Often, we think that we are more than ready to step up when in reality there is likely so much more to learn and grow in. There is also much joy to be found in the fact that we can learn as we go. If you believe you are headed to the office of a prophet, then it is even wiser to take time to be trained, and trained well. Taking the time to understand the order of how things work in this office helps you to not overstep your authority and make a fool of yourself.

A private in the military would never act and operate like a sergeant or a general because there are levels of training, responsibility, and function that come with greater ranks. The same concept is true in the prophet's office and calling. A person does not just decide to be general. It is a long road of successfully passing tests, requirements, and time spent in the trenches.

In the time of the Old Testament prophets, like Samuel, Nathan, and Elijah, there were senior or higher ranking prophets of their day. Having a higher rank does not mean that you can operate at greater levels of prophetic insight and gifts or go into deeper spiritual realms and experiences. It simply, but importantly, means you have greater wisdom and skill on when and how to operate in them. Recognize that rankings also mean you carry a greater level of accountability and responsibility to God for how you've managed what's been placed in your care.

Elisha told the sons of the prophets in Bethel and Jericho to be quiet when they wanted to pronounce their accurately discerned word of knowledge. Although they had rightly discerned the word, they were not yet aware that they were not operating with the higher perspective Elisha had. They had their eyes on Elijah's departure while Elisha had his eyes on Elijah's ascension and his double portion. While Elisha was Elijah's student, he clearly outranked the sons of the prophets in Bethel and Jericho when he told them to be quiet on the matter.

Like the sons of the prophets, a word of knowledge seems to be the novelty of our generation. It's easy to get a couple of prophetic words or predictions correct, and allow pride to dictate that we are further along and deserving of more opportunity and recognition than we currently have. But, like Elisha, wisdom will recognize the journey of being discipled and submit to those mentoring us, being faithful to where God has placed us. Elisha repeated that he would not leave Elijah, and he proved faithful to his mentoring season.

Be content in your season of preparation, no matter how long it may appear to last. There will come a day when it's your turn to pick up the mantle, but you have to ask yourself, "Am I ready? Is the work so solidly in place in my life that I can be found trustworthy?" It's much better to submit to the process than wish that you had when it is too late. Guard your heart from lusting after recognition and position when you think you deserve it.

Understand the stages of the development process you are in. It is important for you to grasp development. It will help to set some of your expectations to a more realistic level. In the kingdom, position comes with greater responsibility and weighty accountability, not just to our mentors and leaders, but to God Himself.

Jesus said, "For everyone to whom much is given, from him much will be required; and to whom much has been committed, of him they will ask the more" (Luke 12:48).

It comes down to the fact that your fruit will speak clearly for itself. It will be obvious to those with discernment if you've let the process of training shape you or if you've taken the easy road and lack the character to sustain the gift. It's important to focus on the stages of maturity in a prophet's development, thus shedding light on the spheres of influence that result with each progression.

GIFT AWARENESS

As a young prophet, you are aware of your calling and your gifts. This is an exciting stage as you are being awakened to a whole new world of fascinating gifts in the spiritual world. You do not know much about how it all works, but you know enough to start operating in aspects of the prophetic.

Maybe it's dreams, visions, visitations, spiritual hearing, or sensory aspects. You have little experience or wisdom here, although you have so little you do not realize that you are lacking in this area. Look for and pursue mature prophets who will be open to mentor you and give you guidance in your gifting and call. It's so important you do this early on, so you do not need to unlearn bad habits down the road of your journey.

NOVICE PROPHET

Being a novice prophet is an extremely enjoyable season as you learn, experiment, and start to explore how your gifts work and function. Each of us has our own unique gifting and spiritual language with the Holy Spirit, so this is not a formula but an organic discovery. We make a lot of mistakes in this season, which is okay. The kingdom is a safe place for the enthusiastic and humble to get it wrong as we grow and test out our spiritual wings. Take your mistakes and learn from them and become wiser every time you find out what doesn't work. Staying hungry for more in humility accelerates your growth.

Study and learn as much as you can about the prophetic and office of the prophet in this season of your life. Learn the Bible inside out, for it will ground you as you grow and set healthy boundaries for you so that you do not minister outside of the Word or nature of God later in life.

AMATEUR PROPHET

You are now growing in skill level of the giftings you have been given. You are starting to become more confident in your giftings and abilities. You are also starting to tap into and discover other gifts and spiritual access that you were not aware of at first. An important key here is to stay humble. A little knowledge and success, the taste of spiritual power flowing through you, can be equally dangerous as it can be beneficial if it is handled incorrectly.

Use this season to master the sword skills of your gifting and, even more importantly, your partnership and relationship with the Holy Spirit. I remember this season very well—fun weeknights would be praying in tongues with my on-fire and hungry friends, and we would go out in a car and drive around the city or up the coast praying in the Holy Spirit for a few hours. During that time, I would always be looking in the Spirit for insight from God around what we were praying over or for a particular detail that God wanted to show us. Sometimes, it was for breakthrough and deliverance over the church or a city, while at other times it was to contend for promises or to see God's plans unfolding. One of my favorite things to do - and still is- at the end of those nights was to ask God to show me insight or a prophetic word of encouragement over each of the people who were with me on that drive.

Prophecy is such a powerful encourager and clarifier. It was a lot of fun, and, at the same time, I used this season to really sharpen my gift in this area. I would close my eyes and look past the blackness of my eyelids into the realm of the Spirit for what God wanted to do or say. Sometimes I would get words and other times visions. All the same, I would spend a great deal of time double checking with God that it was Him giving me the message and not my imagination. This is a huge challenge in the early stages of your development, but as you practice and grow in your skill, you will become well-acquainted with His voice and communication in this area.

Once I felt I had a message from God, I would tell the person it was intended for that I believed God had shown me something for them. I would be able to tell if what was coming out of my mouth was actually God, as I would experience a strong presence of God approving what was being said. If I ever felt an empty flatness and absence of God's presence, I would double check if the word was God's actual word over that person. I trained myself not to fear asking God again. If I was wrong or inaccurate, I would just apologize to the person and retract what I was saying. It's a great safe place to learn. Better to make these mistakes in a car or standing in a room with friends than have to tell your church mid-prophecy, as you stand up from the pulpit, that you are wrong and it's not a message from God.

This is an important phase and season of learning—not a season of recognition. In this season, my mentor had full access to give me feedback about my prophetic progress. While it wasn't always pleasant to receive this feedback, it gave me a sobriety that I was being watched and trained and that my submission to the process was only for my betterment.

Stay humble. Remember David was faithful to his assigned serving role as a shepherd and killed the lion and also a bear in this type of preparation season. Be content here, for ambition will taint your purity and cause you to resent the opportunity you have. Increased mentoring and accountability are paramount at this stage of your prophetic growth.

JUNIOR PROPHET

At this stage of your prophetic journey, you are becoming prophetically trustworthy around your peers. As you have increased in trust, discerning people will give you more opportunity as you become more accurate and walk in maturity in other areas of your life. Remember credibility and integrity are not just how well and accurate you can prophesy—walking with purity, humility, and integrity in all facets of life, and not just in the prophetic, define maturity and trustworthiness. You will be tested in this by the Lord and those who are discerning in leadership.

As you grow, develop, and become more trustworthy, you may be asked to assist at a small group or in a serving capacity at your church using one or more of your gifts. Another area that prophets are extremely valuable to the kingdom is on the church or ministry evangelism team. Serving in this capacity humbly and faithfully without looking for position or recognition is a wise way to gain trust over time with your local leadership.

As you're faithful with the little you have been given, you will start to be trusted with more. This phase of growth will start to display some powerful prophetic giftings. You'll become familiar to the leadership teams as you serve; however, be aware that you will most likely have areas of experience and essential wisdom still lacking. It's essential to remember that while your gifts increase, you do not yet have what's required to move toward more public levels of function.

LOCAL OR RESIDENT PROPHET

Depending on the culture of your local church community, once you have established a track record of prophetic integrity, accuracy, and an honoring submission to those in leadership, you may be invited to function prophetically in your local church. As you are faithful in this new role, you will become more trusted and established within that community. This will make way for promotion and position within the leadership of the church as you are invited by the senior role in place.

The higher you are promoted and utilized in the kingdom, the lower you must bow in humility. The greater people applause the accuracy of your gift, the less you must associate your own abilities and acknowledge it is all Gods' Spirit flowing through you. Do this and you will have longevity in your calling. This is an extremely important reason why young prophets must take significant amount of time in the preparation phases of their call and gift. It's not to emphasize control or restriction, but rather to make room for development, submission to God and authority, mentoring discipleship, and learning humility.

That is why this passage is so imperative to understand around the first four phases of this progression: he must not be "a novice, lest being puffed up with pride he fall into the same condemnation as the devil" (1 Timothy 3:6).

Paul addresses the church, specifically in the aspect of discerning those whom we allow to minister into our own lives: "And we urge you, brethren, to recognize those who labor among you, and are over you in the Lord and admonish you, and to esteem them very highly in love for their work's sake. Be at peace among yourselves" (1 Thessalonians 5:12-13).

I have seen many instances where people allow random strangers to minister in their churches without any testing or relationship. Even worse is when we live in a culture where people's gifts are activated but not matured. Strangers, the rebellious and the lone-ranger types, walk into churches not knowing anyone and assume the right to prophesy over anyone present, without making themselves known or asking the pastoral team. I do not allow this in my church. My role is to protect my people from others who have not been yet proven trustworthy. I have seen one rogue prophetic word do massive damage far too many times from these types of unsubmitted so-called prophets.

A true local or resident prophet is in relationship with the church team and congregation or has been invited in by leadership. It's important that you are known by the leadership and are invited into ministry opportunities—never just assume a place.

At this new level of serving, there is so much more to learn and many more personal and ministerial developmental opportunities. Remember that each new position and opportunity you attain is another depth of learning and requirement. It offers the ability to function and flourish in your gift and role. With that also comes the challenges of the new requirements you will discover. By this stage, you should be beginning to mentor young prophets with the wisdom and progress you have attained thus far.

CITYWIDE PROPHET

Proving faithful in your local church as a prophet will cause you to become established and reliable in the role of the prophet. This stage and every other one that follows is not meant for every prophet. This is an important point to recognize and accept. Trying to network our way into position is a tragic avoidance and denial of allowing and trusting God to promote us in due time. It's really the ultimate act of pride and reliance in our own strength and abilities.

If you end up ministering to your city, region, nation, or even globally, do yourself a huge service and ensure God put you there, and not good marketing. The psalmist said, "For exaltation comes neither from the east nor from the west nor from the south. But God is the Judge: He puts down one, and exalts another" (Psalm 75:6-7).

Each time God enlarges your influence, you must become more heightened in your scrutiny to walk and minister with purity and accuracy. The higher the level of influence, the greater the ability to lead people toward the plans and heart of God, but you also have a greater ability to taint or hurt people. Ensure every word that comes out of your mouth in ministry has a beneficial purpose. Remain soft in your heart, open to correction, and, above all else, guard your heart and what you are allowing to take root there.

REGIONAL, STATEWIDE, NATIONAL, OR GLOBAL SENIOR PROPHET

I have included all three of these rankings and positions in the same point, but these each have their own level of progressive promotion in their stated order. This one is extremely weighty, and simply going on an international ministry trip as a prophet does not put you into this role. If you arrive to the global office, it will be well established and endorsed by heaven and many other ministers.

It is God who must open these doors, as none of us should want to stand in a purpose to which we were not called. As with the citywide prophet, the regional, national, and global prophets will encounter greater levels of accountability and critiques from those who oppose this office. This must be something that is grown into, which usually takes place over a significant period of time. For these higher profile roles, God will normally align you in intimate relationship with someone already standing in these global roles for a significant season. These types of fathering roles are lifelong.

Prophets who stand in these roles are weighty watchmen. These cannot be people pleasers, and so they are not always in popular ministry circles. These individuals are required to have a voice into the direction, standards, and culture of the church so that it follows the paths and ways of God, not straying away from the truth. These prophets will declare regional promises and new things that God wants to do, equally correcting when needed. Usually these individuals have a much clearer understanding of what is taking place in the spiritual realm and will communicate with the heavenly realm on depths that can be unusual to most other believers.

ALLOW GOD TO PROMOTE YOU

Do not be overly ambitious about the level of authority, influence, or position God has entrusted you with. Not many get to the higher ranks, actually fulfilling God's plan. Many get to higher positions in our generation more by association with certain ministers, ministries, and camps, along with good marketing. By doing so, they overstep God's plan and timing. This type of promotion is not recognized in heaven even though many may celebrate it and welcome it in the church on earth. We are called to walk humbly before our King and allow Him to open the right doors and opportunities at the right time. If God isn't giving them the place, do they really have it?

If the enemy cannot stop you growing, then his second greatest strategy is to push you higher than you are equipped to handle. I have seen many who are strong enough in their own personal gifts, determination, willpower, and charm, stand in positions they were not called to or ready for. They may be able to function for a season— maybe even an extended season—but ultimately, the minister gets burned out, sells out, or gets destroyed, and many people are hurt in the process. It is not fitting for an untrained and unwise person to gain the influence, respect, and trust of innocent believers, all to fulfill a selfish ego. If they are promoting themselves into a position, then they are just like the devil—trying to be God to people.

There is always pain and shipwreck when individuals lust and strive toward higher recognition for a gift that they never paid any price for. Gift are just that—gifts. A tool given and entrusted by God for the reverent stewarding of His people. Never allow social media or even those who are enamored by your gifting cause you to lose your humility or sense of submission to God's perfect plan and timing. Remember, there are some doors you are not meant to go through. And there are some that you are.

If God raises you, ensure your humility bows authentically lower with every level of promotion. Never seek the applause of people; always crave the approval of God. Always remember that this generation seeks influence, but the sons and daughters of the kingdom seek intimacy with the King, above all else, pleasing Him and fulfilling His plan. Just like Jesus.

The gift you have, you did not invent or create—you are trusted with it. The same is true about the influence and position you stand in at any given time. God has a pretty clear opinion about who the glory belongs to: "I am the Lord, that is My name; and My glory I will not give to another, nor My praise to carved images" (Isaiah 42:8).

A WORD TO THE READER

I am sure this volume has hit many points for you to consider. My hope is that you, as a prophet, have recognized yourself in the pages. My prayer is that you take this teaching and apply it to every aspect of not only your prophetic life but your life as a whole. I trust that the keys God revealed will act as stepping stones leading you to the fulfillment of God's call over your life. I pray they will give you insight and perspective to embrace who you are as a prophet, as well as insight to see warning signs that may mean that you need to make adjustments.

I believe God has put this book into your hand for a reason. I want to personally thank you for investing your time into this volume. I know that if you embrace the revelations within you will surely make yourself of great use to God, His people, and His kingdom.

THE PROPHETIC TRAINING SERIES:

VOL. I — THE FOUNDATIONS OF THE PROPHETIC

VOL. II — THE PROCESS OF THE PROPHETIC

VOL. III — THE OFFICE OF THE PROPHET

VOL. IV — THE EQUIPMENT OF THE PROPHET

VOL. V — THE PITFALLS OF THE PROPHETIC

VOL. VI — THE ESSENTIALS OF THE PROPHET

VOL. VII — THE NEMESIS OF THE PROPHET

JOIN THE GUILD OF THE PROPHETS

Prophets need prophets; in fact, we should not isolate ourselves from others in the prophetic community. I want to encourage you to sign up and join the Guild of the Prophets. In joining the Guild, you will be encouraged, strengthened, and informed of additional prophetic resources, special pricing, and limited-access events that may be of interest to you. Membership is free.

Look out for the other titles coming soon in the Guild of the Prophets series. This prophetic equipping series has been designed as a school of the prophets, meant to help you grow, develop, and mature into the fullness of your calling in this amazing ministry of expressing God's heart to the world.

Order the series today and receive a discounted package price. Please follow us on Facebook and sign up for e-mail updates about upcoming books and events at www.andrewbillings.org or www.theprophetsguild.com.

ANDREWBILLINGS.ORG

GUILDOFTHEPROPHETS.COM

FIVEFOLD.SCHOOL

AUTHOR BIO

From the time Andrew Billings reconnected with God, in his powerful encounter mentioned in the biography found in volume 2, he served significantly in his local church over many years, in any way that was presented or asked of him, ushering, setting up chairs and equipment for church services, and often traveling with his senior pastor to various nations. He also served as an armor bearer. Andrew firmly believes that this long season of serving was one of the key preparation ingredients that God orchestrated into his life to impart kingdom principles into the core of his DNA.

Andrew firmly believes that leaders are servants. And much of this serving, over twenty years in Andrews life prior to any leadership or ministry, caused him to see ministry not as a noted hierarchy, but as an honorary opportunity to serve and grow others' lives.

Andrew's heart for you as you read through this volume, is that you would take the time to not only master the skill sets of a prophet, but that you would discover the heart of a true prophet. A heart that is fashioned and shaped like the heart of God's, truly caring for people and the things that matter to God.

··· NEXT IN THE SERIES ···

GUILD OF THE PROPHETS

THE EQUIPMENT

OF THE PROPHET

VOL. IV

YOU WILL LEARN ABOUT:

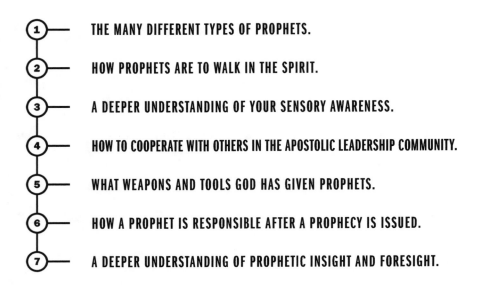

1 — THE MANY DIFFERENT TYPES OF PROPHETS.

2 — HOW PROPHETS ARE TO WALK IN THE SPIRIT.

3 — A DEEPER UNDERSTANDING OF YOUR SENSORY AWARENESS.

4 — HOW TO COOPERATE WITH OTHERS IN THE APOSTOLIC LEADERSHIP COMMUNITY.

5 — WHAT WEAPONS AND TOOLS GOD HAS GIVEN PROPHETS.

6 — HOW A PROPHET IS RESPONSIBLE AFTER A PROPHECY IS ISSUED.

7 — A DEEPER UNDERSTANDING OF PROPHETIC INSIGHT AND FORESIGHT.